ENDORSEM

Shawn Bolz is one of the most "naturally supernatural" people I know and his new book reflects that wonderful balance. You will hunger for more of Jesus and His purposes as you read this book.

—CHE AHN
Senior Pastor, Harvest Rock Church, Pasadena, California

God has gifted Shawn Bolz with understanding, revelation, and application concerning Kingdom finances, which makes this a unique and urgent book for the Body of Christ today. We desperately need to understand and apply these principles so that Jesus will receive the fullness of His inheritance. This book is a divine invitation for those who are ready, willing to pay the price, and waiting to partner with Him for the critical times ahead.

—JILL AUSTIN
President and Founder, Master Potter Ministries

Amazing encounters! Amazing understanding! Amazing revelatory teaching! This is not just another good book—it contains part of Heaven's blueprint for abundant provision for God's end-time purposes. Read, believe, prepare, and receive. Within these pages awaits an appointment with destiny, with you in mind!

—JAMES W. GOLL
Cofounder, Encounters Network

Understanding the heart and ways of God concerning Kingdom economy is wonderfully disclosed in this vision. In *Keys to Heaven's Economy*, Shawn Bolz faithfully stewards a profound and divine prophetic revelation. If his vision and teaching are received in faith, the reader will definitely be impacted and blessed as I was.

—PATRICIA KING
Founder, Extreme Prophetic

This revelation, given by way of visitation to Shawn Bolz, will operate with a breaker anointing to release faith and hope to individuals as they read. It felt alive and as if the Heavens were being opened up for provision on my behalf; my understanding turned into expectation. I thank God for ones like Shawn who have given themselves to the Lord in such a way as to receive deep spiritual understanding for the Body of Christ.

—JOANN MCFATTER
Founder, Inside-Eternity
www.joannmcfatter.com

In *Keys to Heaven's Economy*, Shawn Bolz reveals to us the Lord's desire to bless us and bring us into a full manifestation of His resources. We are entering into the next phase of the supernatural war over the *transference of wealth*. Shawn gives us great insight into this dimension of Kingdom exchange.

—DR. CHUCK D. PIERCE
President, Glory of Zion International Ministries, Inc.
Vice President, Global Harvest Ministries

This book will cause your heart to tremble with a renewed awareness of the sacredness of all God has entrusted to you. Especially fascinating is Shawn Bolz's insight on how God's strategy is to deploy His fivefold ministry giftings into all levels of the business and professional sectors.

—BOB SORGE
Author and Teacher, www.oasishouse.net

KEYS TO HEAVEN'S ECONOMY

An Angelic Visitation
from the Minister *of* Finance

SHAWN BOLZ

Streams Publishing House
North Sutton, New Hampshire

Published by Streams Publishing House, a division of Streams
Ministries International™, P.O. Box 550, North Sutton, New
Hampshire 03260
World Wide Web: www.streamsministries.com

To contact the author about speaking at your conference or church,
please go to www.whitedoveministries.org.

Managing Editor and Creative Director: Carolyn Blunk
Contributing Editor: Dorian Kreindler
Associate Editor: Lauren Stinton
Assistant Editor: Mary Ballotte
Editorial Assistant: Leslie Herrier
Cover design by Mike Bailey
Interior design by Pat Reinheimer

ISBN: 1-58483-102-2

Library of Congress
2005934411

Printed in the United States of America.

FOR MORE INFORMATION
ON STREAMS BOOKS AND OTHER MATERIALS,
CALL 1.888.441.8080 (USA AND CANADA)
OR 603.927.4224

OTHER BOOKS BY SHAWN BOLZ

The Throne Room Company

For Guy Charles Bolz, my older brother,
whose brief earthly life profoundly influenced mine.
You became the spiritual seed planted in the ground
giving life to our entire family.
I look forward to spending an eternity with you.

This book is also dedicated to my friend Carolyn Blunk,
who is in eternity now. She sacrificed her own projects to help
birth the writing of many, including this book, which she labored
for as if it came from her own experience. Every life this book
impacts will be added to her eternal inheritance.

CONTENTS

FOREWORD

L   ike its author, *Keys to Heaven's Economy* is inspiring,
     prophetic, and powerful. I have known Shawn since
     he was fifteen years old. He is a passionate pursuer of
God, and I have been greatly encouraged by his prophetic
insights and supernatural revelations over the years.

Shawn represents a new breed of revolutionary lovers of
God, individuals who sacrifice earthly rewards so they may
share in Heaven's heartbeat. As such, Shawn has set his
heart "on things above" (Colossians 3:1) rather than on
earthly things.

In these amazing encounters, Shawn takes us with him as
he is visited several times by an angel called the Minister of
Finance for the Kingdom. The revelations are stunning and
challenging. They provoke a response that can at times be
uncomfortable but is necessary as we open ourselves to be
changed more into the likeness of Jesus Christ.

Get ready to be touched by God through this book. In a
world that operates in a "what's in it for me" mentality, Shawn
offers us the challenge to consider, "What's in it for God?"

I am convinced the revelation in this book will set many free and will be used to change the destiny of millions. May your reading of this book bring you further along in your spiritual walk and help you find God's purpose for you in His Kingdom.

JOHN PAUL JACKSON
Founder, Streams Ministries International

Introduction

When you have supernatural encounters with the Lord Jesus or with heavenly beings who belong to Him, it is hard to know how to steward their revelations adequately. Do you tell others about them? If so, when and how?

When I first described over the Internet my visitation from an angel called the Minister of Finance, I received thousands of e-mails from people hungry to know more. Readers were especially touched by the reality that God is about to release finances and resources to reshape the Body of Christ on the earth, spilling over the walls of current religious structures. People were encouraged to learn that Heaven's angels long to partner with humans to bring Jesus what rightfully belongs to Him.

I felt a great responsibility to write this revelation down, even though it would entail sharing very personal encounters and words that were originally geared toward only a few individuals and myself. As this revelation unfolded and further visitations happened, I realized this insight was for the whole Body of Christ.

We are coming into a season in which spiritual commissioning to a secular job is as important as a full-time ministry. Those in secular positions must have the same intensity of calling as those who have received a mandate for church ministry.

God desires for this generation to infiltrate every secular industry so He can manifest and receive His glory. He has also purposed to grow a godly counterculture in the midst of the world system. Being part of a godly counterculture is a dangerous occupation since the Antichrist spirit has overwhelmed earthly systems to the point of domination. But where darkness is, greater light will come.

"Arise, shine;
For your light has come!
And the glory of the LORD is risen upon you.
For behold, the darkness shall cover the earth,
And deep darkness the people;
But the LORD will arise over you,
And His glory will be seen upon you.
The Gentiles shall come to your light,
And kings to the brightness of your rising."
—ISAIAH 60:1–3, NKJV

In this very hour, God has a mandated release of resources and finances to be invested in the men and women who would use them for His Kingdom's advancement. This supply is slated for those who would stand up in this generation, no matter the cost, and deliver to Jesus everything they can steward—His reward and inheritance.

Over the past few years, I have had what I believe to be a profound series of revelations regarding the Son's spiritual inheritance that the Father wants to manifest on earth as it is in Heaven.

In order for God's Kingdom dominion to be realized, we must experience a paradigm shift. God has used my prophetic journey to explain many things to me—life becomes not just a series of events but a deliberate unfolding of tangible, divine purposes shown in a visible way. I would like to recount some of these personal experiences and even family history with you. As you read these accounts, please fully open your heart to the Holy Spirit.

May this book be a resource to inspire you to a higher understanding of God's end-time focus. God will release many to reap the ripened harvest, which comprises not just the salvation of souls but also Jesus' Kingdom actively being released over all the face of the earth and gaining dominion over the hearts of humanity.

For some, this book will provide more support for what God has revealed to you concerning your role in His Kingdom on the earth. For others, it will serve as new and fresh revelation.

Whichever is true for you, I pray that as you read this book, my experiences and insights will spark greater vision to ignite your faith, expand your hope, and unfold God's design of your eternal destiny.

CHAPTER ONE

RESTORING DESOLATE INHERITANCES

May [they] be encouraged in heart and united in love, so that they may have the full riches of complete understanding, in order that they may know the mystery of God, namely, Christ, in whom are hidden all the treasures of wisdom and knowledge.

—COLOSSIANS 2:2–3

All the sun's intensity seemed to blaze through my bedroom window that morning of July 5, 2001. The sun's rising was so brilliant that I turned the other way to avoid it, but as I rolled over, mirrors reflected the light straight into my eyes. Blinded from both sides, I sat up, squinted, and looked down at the edge of my bed. What I saw stunned me: A man stood there watching me.

I studied him for a few seconds and realized he was not a human being but an angel who carried the very atmosphere of Heaven—and not just any angel, but one of Heaven's great angelic beings. I had never had an experience quite like this, and the fear of the Lord gripped my heart.

Although this angel carried an air of nobility, he was dressed rather humbly in a brown robe that looked like burlap. It was covered with pockets. Beneath the robe was another garment that appeared translucent and alive, much like living light.

The angel was approximately six feet tall with brown hair and piercing hazel eyes, which I wanted to avoid looking into because I was frightened by the intensity of the love and authority they conveyed. At the same time, I couldn't seem to take away my gaze—we were totally eye-locked. His face radiated both compassion and authority. Suddenly, I understood why John the Beloved had become confused and worshipped an angel who had appeared to him (Revelation 19:10), because angels foreshadow God's radiant and luminous appearance.

THE VOICE OF THE LORD

Before I could say anything, the Lord's audible voice filled the room, introducing the angel standing before me: "Welcome the Minister of Finance of the Kingdom."

The sound was both a trumpet and a voice in one. Waves of the Lord's presence rippled through me. Later, I found out that a young boy in the next room had been awakened and terrified by the audible voice of God. After the Lord's announcement, He continued speaking to me internally through my spirit, giving me greater understanding about this angel and his high-ranking position.

Immediately, I knew this angel had command over all the finances and resources that heavenly authority calls forth from earth. These resources have only one purpose: to bring Jesus His full reward and inheritance in our age. What a holy and noble occupation this angel had! No wonder I felt God's glory in the room as the angel stood there.

The angelic Minister of Finance began to walk around the foot of the bed, heading toward me. As he did, I thought, *Why me? Why here?* But before I go further, I must share some circumstances surrounding my trip to California that will help you more fully understand this angelic visitation from Heaven's throne room.

CHAPTER TWO

DISCOVERING MY INHERITANCE

I pray also that the eyes of your heart may be enlightened in order that you may know the hope to which he has called you, the riches of his glorious inheritance in the saints, and his incomparably great power for us who believe.

—EPHESIANS 1:18–19

B efore I was born, my parents lost a child. His name was Guy Charles Bolz and he was only four years old when he died. Although my parents were not Christians at the time, Guy had an all-consuming love for God. As a small child, he talked about God and Jesus all the time; he was a joy to everyone he met. In some ways, Guy was a martyr for our family, since it was after his unsuccessful fight with leukemia that my parents sought Jesus.

Even in Guy's death there was a supernatural occurrence. In the middle of a bone-marrow transplant, he died on the operating table. When the doctor came to find my parents in the waiting room, they knew the worst had happened and began to sob.

Suddenly, a woman with an extraordinary countenance appeared in the waiting room. She carried an atmosphere of peace and brought immediate comfort to my mother, who had never before experienced such profound grief. This glorious woman sat with my parents for a while and then left.

Later, as my parents talked about the experience, it seemed that both had seen an entirely different woman in appearance—different hair and dress—yet they were sitting next to each other the entire time. The presence of love that rested upon this woman caused their hearts to ache for God. After realizing the woman was an angel the Lord had sent at my brother's passing, they ended up finding God.

In addition to my older sister, Cindy, my mother later gave birth to two more children—my sister, Jennifer, and me. All of us carried a hole in our hearts for our brother, who had left us so long ago. Although he had died before my birth, my heart yearned to know him.

DISCOVERING MY INHERITANCE

In 2000, God began to speak to me about the call on my brother's life. He told me that Guy's life had been taken prematurely. This confirmed something in our hearts, since we had always felt that he should still have been alive. We felt incomplete, as if a part of the family was missing in some way.

God revealed there was an inheritance for me to receive—the calling Guy would have walked in. God was now asking me to claim it.

I saw a picture in which I was holding a claim ticket in my hands for the things Jesus had had in His heart for my brother to walk out on this earth. I began to call forth that inheritance of destiny and gifting. As I did, God healed the hole in my heart for my brother by enlarging my heart to receive the love and calling Guy would have walked out. Several years before, a prophetic man who hadn't known about my brother had given me this very word, but it had never been impressed upon my heart or made sense until this moment.

During the season in which God was unraveling these revelations about my brother, I was visiting friends in California, and my parents happened to be visiting friends in Washington state. We had not talked in several days, but God put them on my heart. One night, I went to bed early, and I had a powerful dream about them that felt like it lasted the entire night. It was a dream that used my brother in a symbolic way for our family.

A DREAM ABOUT GUY'S RESURRECTION

In this dream, I watched a grave keeper doing lawn work at a graveyard in Washington state. He came across a grave that had been completely dug up, and a little boy was standing beside the open coffin. The startled grave keeper asked, "Little boy, where are your parents?" But the child didn't know.

"Where did you last see them?"

"In the hospital," the little boy answered.

Nervously, the grave keeper asked, "What is your name?"

The little boy replied, "Guy Charles Bolz."

The grave keeper looked at the tombstone and noticed the boy's name was engraved there. (In the natural, my brother is buried in Washington state, just as in this dream.)

"Now, this isn't funny, young man," the grave keeper said. "Where are your parents?" He began to look around frantically, unsure who would put such a young child up to this prank. But it wasn't a prank.

The little boy replied, "I don't know where they are. But I was in Heaven with Jesus, and He asked me to go to my parents; they needed me."

The grave keeper's expression revealed his shock and awe. He didn't know what to do, so he took the little boy to his office and instructed him to wait while he called for help. The grave keeper didn't know whom to call, so he pressed zero for an operator.

A woman's voice came on the line, and as he began to tell her what had happened, she proclaimed, "God has raised him from the dead. I must find his parents! Praise Jesus!"

The grave keeper had not been expecting to talk to a Christian. This was too much for the poor man, and he just slumped down in the chair while she got in contact with the parents.

The scene changed, and I saw my parent's house in Kansas City; suddenly, their phone rang. My mom was in the kitchen, and my dad was in the living room. My dad answered the phone next to him.

"Is this Larry Bolz?" a woman asked. He confirmed that it was.

"Did you have a son who passed away at the age of four?" she asked.

"Yes," he answered. His firstborn son had died at a young age.

"I don't know how to explain this to you," she said, "but we have your son on the line. He is alive!"

In unbelief and anger, my dad asked her, "Is this a sick joke? He has been dead for years!"

She assured him that it wasn't a joke or prank. Still, my

dad was about to hang up until he heard a little voice: "Daddy? Daddy, is that you?" I saw my dad's shocked face; his broken heart began beating. It was the son he had lost! He recognized the voice. "Guy?" he asked, mystified.

At this point, my mother, who had overheard the conversation, jumped on another phone in the house. "Who is this?" she asked.

She heard the giggle of a son who had been long gone and her heart was pierced by it. "Guy?" she asked eagerly.

"Yes, Mommy. Jesus brought me back to you! I'm alive!"

My parents and Guy all began to cry. There couldn't have been a happier reunion.

I awoke from the dream sobbing so hard from the full mental picture of my parents weeping as they heard their firstborn son's voice one more time.

"Oh, God, what is this?" I asked in the midst of my weeping.

In my spirit, I heard Him respond, "I am taking your parents back to America's northwest region. When they go, everything that I have promised them that may seem dead and long buried is going to be resurrected. The full purpose of their lives will be accomplished!"

A RESURRECTION ANOINTING

I was amazed by this revelation and how it came. My parents are mature Christians who have had many promises given to them. For several years, they had believed God would use them in a significant way for His Kingdom. But as the years went by, every promise seemed to drift further and further away. They were not wasting time by any means, but certain promises had never come to them and would take the complete hand of God to fulfill.

My parents had spent many years immersed in the armed forces, serving God and country. My father is a retired colonel in the U.S. Air Force, and he and my mother were feeling older. They had given up going to the nations long ago, discarding hopes of taking their writing, singing, and healing gifts abroad. Now, Jesus was resurrecting their callings and promises. He was comparing the destiny on their lives to the precious son they had lost—they would experience a resurrection of something that had died long ago. He would do this by His power and leading.

I waited until I was home from California to relate the dream to them. I shared that God was going to move them back to the Northwest to claim their full inheritance. We cried together as I shared how God was entrusting this calling to them in the same way He had entrusted their hearts to Guy. Their affection for God's calling on their lives would be just as real as if Guy were resurrected and standing before them.

God wants to take many people through this resurrection process. He wants to bring to life divine promises that we have placed on the altar and killed. It is time for our faith to be stirred again. God is going to bring a resurrection anointing to us. It will come first to dreams that have died, and it will end in a manifestation of true resurrection anointing.

CLAIMING MY SPIRITUAL INHERITANCE

A year later, in June 2001, God told two friends and me to go to California. I was excited to go back to my homeland because of my deep love for it. A dear friend of mine, Jill Austin, was going to speak at a conference in Lancaster and asked if I wanted to come. Instantly, I heard the Lord: It was *not* an option—I was going.

I called my parents and discovered they were going to Spokane, Washington. I asked when they were leaving, and it turned out to be the same morning I was leaving for California.

"What time are you leaving, Mom?" I asked.

"Nine thirty a.m. on Southwest Airlines," she replied.

"I'm leaving at nine thirty-three on Southwest for California! God is telling me to go get an inheritance of promise, but I don't know why He picked the place we are going."

"Where are you going?" she asked.

"Lancaster," I responded. There was dead silence on the other end. Then my mother began to cry.

"Shawn, that is where your brother, Guy, was born," she said between sobs.

I had never known where he was born; we were an Air Force family and moved all my life. We never really talked about his birth. I was undone—my parents were going to the Northwest to claim what God had given us in the dream about my brother, and at the same time, I was going to Guy's birthplace to claim an inheritance. God is so amazing!

So on that morning in July 2001 (mentioned in Chapter One), I understood why God had the Minister of Finance visit me while I was staying in Lancaster. The angel was coming to release to me part of my brother's spiritual inheritance. I felt the holiness of the moment.

RESTORING SPIRITUAL INHERITANCES

This is what the LORD says:
"In the time of my favor I will answer you,
and in the day of salvation I will help you;

I will keep you and will make you
to be a covenant for the people,
to restore the land
and to reassign its desolate inheritances."

—ISAIAH 49:8

Literally, there are spiritual inheritances and assignments that have been abandoned and unfulfilled—but are available to be picked up again. In the days ahead, the Lord is going to direct many on how to access these unused treasures. There is an appointed time of favor that comes in the day of salvation— a designated time when the Father is investing into Jesus' very inheritance.

We need to understand the concept of the unfinished commissions lying idle in the spirit realm that are waiting to be picked up by those who have a right to them. Sometimes these mandates are unfinished because the person died prematurely; sometimes the person who was walking with the Lord fell into disobedience or sin and left an unfinished assignment. On the other hand, a spiritual inheritance is left behind by those who have gone on to be with the Lord. God wants to open our spiritual eyes to see our divine birthright to the spiritual inheritances and unfinished commissions surrounding us.

A friend of mine had a very clear revelation of a place where spiritual inheritances from previous generations were chained up and layered in demonic bondage. But he saw that God was about to commission people to go into this spiritual realm and retrieve precious treasures that had been stolen by the enemy.

When people enter eternity, having lived a life of obedience in partnering with God, they leave behind a spiritual inheritance. God is looking for individuals who will pick up these inheritances and walk in the legacy of those who have paved the way ahead.

Divine purposes are like tracks in the spirit realm. God is inviting us onto the tracks that have already been laid, to follow a trail that has already been blazed. If we don't have to create a new track from scratch, we can further advance God's Kingdom. The writer of Hebrews even goes so far to say:

> These were all commended for their faith, yet none
> of them received what had been promised. God had
> planned something better for us so that only
> together with us would they be made perfect.
> —HEBREWS 11:39–40

Some in Heaven have unfulfilled promises. Our participation will allow them to see God's perfect plan unfold. These generational inheritances can affect our finances, resources, ministries, and so much more.

> "It is too small a thing for you to be my servant
> to restore the tribes of Jacob
> and bring back those of Israel I have kept.
> I will also make you a light for the Gentiles,
> that you may bring my salvation to the ends of the earth."
> —ISAIAH 49:6

Isaiah explained how the Lord prepared him for a specific purpose, but because the Lord's favor came upon him, he received an expansion of that purpose. He received a larger portion of stewardship that enabled him to walk in a higher inheritance in Heaven.

STEWARDING GREAT CALLINGS

In this generation, God is inviting us to steward great callings to the ends of the earth. These callings do not just have a church-building focus; they have a secular function as well. Many callings were left unfulfilled because they are to be released to a greater arena—the entire world—and the people walking in them were limited in their identity by the church or ministry.

Some of the greatest mantles and anointings to ever be released on the earth are still available. These are not just for the ministry world. God wants to pour out anointing in every field known to humankind, bringing Him glory and furthering His reward.

Truly, these are among the most exciting days to be called beyond the Church's walls, because God is releasing disciples into every industry and occupation. An anointing is being released to people with secular jobs so they can bring God a harvest just as great—and potentially many times greater—than those in Church ministry. Never has there been a more exciting time for those in secular jobs to enter into a covenantal purpose with God in the Western world.

Since the advent of Christianity, most moves of God have happened within the confines of a church organization. When these moves did extend beyond the reach of the Church, they impacted only thousands, not millions, of people. However, God is going to bring a movement that will result in a cultural shift in the secular arena. This impact will be as profound as Martin Luther's efforts to make the Scriptures available to everyone, not just the religious few. Luther's vision changed cultures globally, and it happened in one generation.

The first time I heard Mike Bickle, founder of the International House of Prayer, speak, I was riveted by his vision. He used a simple statement that shot as an arrow from Heaven into my heart: "God is about to change the face of Christianity in one generation"—*our* generation.

There has been only a handful of times when God changed the face of Christianity in one generation. Each time He did, it affected the secular culture as deeply as Church culture. When there is an agreement between Heaven and earth, everything shifts toward godliness.

CHAPTER THREE

FIRST VISITATION

The LORD is exalted, for he dwells on high;
he will fill Zion with justice and righteousness.
He will be the sure foundation for your times,
a rich store of salvation and wisdom and knowledge;
the fear of the LORD is the key to this treasure.

—ISAIAH 33:5–6

The Minister of Finance was completely silent. He was so quiet that I could hear my heart pounding in my chest. Standing beside my bed, he began to reach into the pockets of his robe and pull out keys. At a supernatural rate of speed, he placed these keys on a key chain, reaching into his pockets twenty times a second and pulling out more keys.

I saw more than a hundred keys. They were too hard to count because it happened so fast. I recall seeing house keys, car keys, office keys, hotel room keys, card keys, window keys, bank keys, safety deposit keys, and many other different types. I even saw some futuristic keys that have not been used yet. After only a few seconds, all the keys had been transferred from his pockets to the supernatural key chain. So many keys fitting on one chain was supernatural in itself.

Then the Minister of Finance reached forward with both hands, placed the key chain on my chest, and pressed on it. As he did, I was stunned, because the key chain passed through my skin as though it were liquid and went inside me. It was like cinematic special effects. I felt the coldness of the metal keys. The hands of the Minister of Finance were icy hot; I felt an electric shock as they touched me. When he lifted his hands, I could see the outline of the keys underneath my skin. Then he pressed them all the way down into my spirit.

Instantly, I had the impression that I was not alone in this experience. I represented many believers who were receiving keys from Heaven to prepare the way of the Lord. These keys would unlock opportunities in the natural that would finance projects for God's Kingdom dominion on the earth.

I saw a vision of this angel going around the world and placing keys in the hands of different people to open doors that had been promised. In particular, I saw three people to whom he had given keys; two of them were already beginning to walk into their promises.

Then the Minister of Finance touched my forehead with his icy-hot fingers, and I saw several other visions.

JESUS WITH THOUSANDS OF KEYS

The first vision was of Jesus standing in the Heavens, looking down upon the earth. He was holding a key chain similar to the one that had melted into my chest, but His key chain was much larger, with hundreds of thousands of keys. He rattled the keys in His hand, and a great thunder was heard in the Heavens as Kingdom activity was announced.

The keys were of all types: to houses, buildings, vehicles of every kind, land titles, technology and science industries, hospitals, movie studios, schools, medical resources, political resources—everything that could be owned and would need a key. I realized these keys would unlock His inheritance on the earth. These keys were for tangible resources that humanity would have stewardship over, bringing Jesus ownership of the souls impacted by the resources.

What an eye-opening experience! This vision made the reality of what Jesus was called to inherit extraordinary in my perspective! There were so many natural things that came under His dominion. Quite honestly, I had never understood that He would be so influential on the earth.

Then Jesus spoke to me, but His mouth never moved: "I am coming with keys to My Kingdom!"

The keys on the chain then sounded like wind chimes—but incredibly intense and loud. Suddenly, I knew that only the Holy Spirit's wind would cause these keys to find their locks and unlock divine promises. A great spiritual understanding hit me: No resource will be spared. Everything will go toward bringing Jesus His full inheritance.

Jesus spoke to His disciples about this realm of authority:

"I will give you the keys of the kingdom of heaven;
whatever you bind on earth will be bound in heaven,
and whatever you loose on earth will be loosed in
heaven."

—MATTHEW 16:19

When we come into agreement with God's purposes, He will release any key we need that will deliver to Jesus what belongs to Him. These keys will lock or unlock the unfolding of the great promise so that the Son of God will reap His full reward. Over the next two years, this vision reccurred several times. As it did, I would literally see keys coming down from Heaven and falling into someone's hand on earth.

On one occasion, I was in Kellogg, Idaho, and Jesus appeared to me in a vision. As the Holy Spirit's wind blew through the keys, two keys were released and were given to someone in ministry; I knew that two buildings would be given to this man. When I shared this prophetic vision with him, he became excited. Since his ministry didn't have finances to buy these buildings, they would have to come as a provision from Heaven. A short time later, the person received a phone call and was given a building for only a few dollars, a laughable amount compared to its market value.

On another occasion, I saw a house key being released to a friend who needed a place to stay. I knew it was a provision for a specific season in my friend's life. The key appeared to her in the natural when some European friends gave her the use of their only American investment. They invited her to live in and steward their home free of charge, making it a retreat and sanctuary, which she has faithfully done.

Another time, a group from the West Coast came to Kansas City's International House of Prayer, hungry to start a house of prayer in their city. As I prayed for them, I saw a key chain released over a group of buildings—a large strip mall. When I shared this, they immediately became excited and explained they had been negotiating the purchase of a strip mall near their church. They had even taken a leap of faith to purchase it. They returned home and were thrilled to learn that the owner had knocked down the price signifi-cantly, for no apparent reason. The owner also began making needed repairs at his own expense!

In another vision, I was taken up California's Highway 405

to Culver City, and I saw one of Hollywood's largest movie studios, one that resembled an enclosed city. The Lord spoke to me: "This was built for Me, and I will possess it." In the vision, the studio complex had large white walls surrounding it and multiple security gates. In the natural, I had never seen a studio. Then one day while I was on a ministry trip in California, I drove to Culver City with some friends to see if we could "walk out" the vision. Stunned, I found the movie studio exactly where I had seen it in the vision. This sparked something inside me regarding what God had shown me and how this studio will impact the world in the years to come.

During a two-year period, God gave me similar visions of keys being released. The Lord showed me more than fourteen buildings that He was giving to individuals and ministries, and all of these buildings have been released, with the exception of the movie studio. These buildings ranged from houses to strip malls, from vacant hospitals to large corporate structures. All are part of what God is reclaiming or building for His Kingdom purposes.

Since that time, God has often shown me buildings with large keys in front of them. As I glance at the doors, I can tell if they are going to be released soon for redemptive purposes. This helps me encourage people about pursuing a specific building.

BAGS OF GOLD

After seeing the vision of Jesus holding thousands of keys, the scene changed, and a second vision appeared.

Suddenly, the Heavens opened above me. The Minister of Finance, who had been standing next to me, ascended. Two angels appeared holding an ark, a type of box resembling a treasure chest. The Minister of Finance stood over these angels. Other angels, whom I knew to be angels of resource, appeared carrying white bags that radiated with heavenly light. Each angel carried two bags full of gold—and not just any gold! Inside these bags were end-time resources to secure Jesus' inheritance.

The Minister of Finance directed the resource angels to unseal the bags of gold. As they began to pour the gold into the treasure chest, they covered it from my view, as if the gold were too holy for me to see. In fact, the holiness of God's glory just on the bags themselves was too powerful and made me look away. Each time I would try and peek, I would get lost in the vision, and the scene would grow so intense, almost like trying to view the sun at noon. I tried to see the wonderful gold that was in the bags, but I was not permitted to, because the bags were marked for extremely holy purposes, and those who looked upon them would be branded with those purposes. So the gold was hidden from my sight.

Four angels were sent to earth with eight bags of gold. They surrounded a sleeping man who suddenly awoke when they entered his room. He was a businessman. As he sat up, the angels laid the bags around him on the bed. A holy hush filled the room. The angels spoke to the faceless businessman, but I couldn't hear what they said.

The man grabbed one of the bags and instantly began to shake as if gripped by a seizure, because the power in the bag was like electric current. I wanted to see what was inside, but again I wasn't permitted to. The man began to open the bag, and as he looked inside, a bright yellow light emerged and illuminated his face.

The moment was so holy that the man began to weep as he saw provision for the very thing God had been calling him to do. Yet it wasn't just provision—he was also imprinted with strategy and understanding about how to steward these finances. He had waited upon the Lord for years and felt the fear of God regarding the release of these great funds.

The angels began to sing around him in exaltation and fellowship, rejoicing that it was time for one more great deposit into a willing and ready vessel. The man just kept weeping with great joy. The weariness of carrying so much purpose without a natural manifestation was removed from him as he received everything he needed in a mere moment.

In this man's case, the gold was released for a hospital project that would bring natural and spiritual healing under one roof. As I watched him crying, I saw the blueprint for this project in his brain. Shortly afterward, he lay back down, crying and thanking God for His provision.

I believe this vision depicts what God wants to do at this moment. The man who was sleeping represented many who are asleep toward their God-given purposes. They are content to live according to our culture's worldview. Because they have not been empowered by God's greater purpose for their lives, they are asleep to the treasures God longs to release.

The angels came and placed bags of gold on this man's bed, which represents an intimate place. Likewise, the great strategies needed by those called to steward resources in the days ahead will *only* come from our spending time with the Lord in intimacy—abiding in Him.

When the man grabbed the bag, he was empowered for the very purpose that was so dear to him. Likewise, many people have an intellectual understanding of their earthly position and function, but great empowerment will come as they touch the holiness of God's awesome, supernatural purpose amidst ordinary life. This represents our need to encounter the Holy Spirit. Revelation came as the man grabbed hold of the bag, and he was shaken.

Then he looked in the bag, and I knew his eyes and vision were purified. The light that threatened to blind me didn't cause him to shield his eyes; he had been purified so that he could see into his purpose with the open eyes of revelation. It would take revelation to steward what he was given. He was equipped for his purpose as this revelation was released and combined with the Holy Spirit's empowerment and divine love.

THE LOCKED DOOR AND
THE RELEASE OF A KEY

The vision changed again, and in this third vision, I watched as a dark-skinned angel entered the inner city of what seemed to be Los Angeles. One of the heavenly keys was blowing in the wind before him. The angel appeared to be following the key, which was for unlocking finances for media, according to God's purposes.

As the key blew with the wind, I expected to see it open doors, but instead, it flew into a man's hand. The angel seemed surprised, too, because he almost ran into him.

The man was holding up his hands, waiting to receive from the Lord, and even though there were several open doors before him, he was focused on one door in the middle that was closed. Not only was it closed, but it was locked, and it seemed to be the most important; there was no way into this opportunity. I realized the locked door was the most costly one—the one this man wanted more than anything. The other doors had easy access and many people had gone through them, but this man wanted to go through the locked door because no one had ever gone through it before.

Just as he was crying out to the Lord one more time, the key fell into his hand. Suddenly, he knew it was time. He looked down at the key and then jumped out of his chair. He was so eager that he violently burst through the locked door at full force!

His actions inspired the angel standing next to me. The angel began to worship, seeing another chosen vessel take what was given by God and use it to its fullest. This man would enter into a divine season of anointing, in which everything he set his hands to would turn into the radiant gold I hadn't been allowed to view in the previous vision.

I knew this man represented many who have not compromised by taking on easy projects leading to quick gain. This man was one who had paid a price. He waited on God daily for the keys to divine promises to come forth. Developing a deeper intimacy with God, the man lifted his hands, waiting as David did:

> Hear my cry for mercy
> as I call to you for help,
> as I lift up my hands
> toward your Most Holy Place.
>
> —PSALM 28:2

God is looking for individuals who are dependent on Him and who are not expecting others to open the doors. He is watching for those who longingly wait for an open-door experience with the One who is the Master of all keys. As the Psalmist writes, such individuals are those whose only hope is in Him:

> I lift up my eyes to the hills—
> where does my help come from?

My help comes from the LORD,
the Maker of heaven and earth.

He will not let your foot slip—
he who watches over you will not slumber;
indeed, he who watches over Israel
will neither slumber nor sleep.

The LORD watches over you—
the LORD is your shade at your right hand;
the sun will not harm you by day,
nor the moon by night.

The LORD will keep you from all harm—
he will watch over your life;
the LORD will watch over your coming and going
both now and forevermore.

—PSALM 121

God is raising up individuals who will carry the full manifestation of His desire. These people will take a leap of faith, in the hope that everything they invest into will prosper and with the goal of delivering to Jesus His great reward. Many men and women anointed of God in every conceivable secular and ministerial job will have counsel from Heaven on how to carry God's desire into their careers.

SOLOMON'S DESIRE TO BUILD

During this particular season of visions, I opened the Bible to read about the life of Solomon. As I did, I had a supernatural experience that divinely illuminated my understanding of the role of this great king. It seemed as if the Holy Spirit was reading to me from the Old Testament books of 1 and 2 Kings and 1 and 2 Chronicles. I began to ponder thoughts about Solomon that only God could have brought to my mind.

I saw that King Solomon walked in a powerful manifestation of God's Spirit with the favor of Heaven—the golden touch. When Solomon built the temple, God wanted it to be a demonstration of the greatest release of agreement between Heaven and earth. God desired a dwelling place on earth, and now humanity desired to build a temple for God.

Because of Solomon's desire stated in 2 Chronicles 2:5, God allowed angels of resource to supply Solomon with the most prestigious materials known in his day: cedars of Lebanon, precious stones, the finest gold from Parvaim, so much bronze that no one was ever able to measure how much was used, purple fabric to make the curtain of the Holy of Holies, the best artisans and builders known on earth at the time, and so much more! This is what a divine release of heavenly resources looks like. I believe that in our generation, God is going to release the best resources known to humanity to accomplish His agenda on earth. As a result, we will see such a scintillating agreement between Heaven and earth that Solomon's temple will be a pale reflection by comparison.

Just as in John 2:10, the Father has saved the best wine for last, and we are about to witness a generation whom God will use to bring the most intense manifestation of Heaven to the earth. While He was among us, Jesus taught us to pray that the Kingdom of Heaven would come to earth (Luke 11:2), because that is God's great desire before the end of this age.

Solomon built the temple in agreement with Heaven. He obtained favor with God, and consequently, he had stewardship over more riches than anyone had before him. Because of divine favor, Solomon "became greater than all the kings of the earth in riches and wisdom" (1 Kings 10:23, NASB).

When God invests in humans, He always has the noblest intentions in His heart. Just as God held nothing back from Solomon, He will hold nothing back from the generation who longs to bring Jesus everything that belongs to Him!

Earthly riches apportioned for a spiritual purpose will be distributed to those who align themselves with Heaven's goals and the flowchart of eternity. These riches cannot be delegated to those who seek their own success and tithe their small percentage on earth. Rather, they will be allotted to those who will live sacrificially, pouring out their costly nard to anoint Jesus' feet and cleansing them with their hair (their glory), those who will give their last mite for the temple offering.

The Holy Spirit will send keys to unlock doors for those consumed with zeal to bring Jesus His full reward; He will reward those who walk the narrow road. This road contains no motives for selfish gain—only the longing to prepare the bride for her wonderful Beloved.

CHAPTER FOUR

THE OPEN HEAVEN

Everyone was filled with awe, and many wonders and miraculous signs were done by the apostles. All the believers were together and had everything in common. Selling their possessions and goods, they gave to anyone as he had need.

—ACTS 2:43–45

A fter this series of visions, the Minister of Finance looked upward, and as I followed his gaze, he flew up and out of the room. My bedroom ceiling disappeared and Heaven opened over me. As I gazed into the open Heavens, I saw awesome visions. I believe that everyone who pursues Heaven according to the Father's desire for His Son needs to cry out to see the Heavens opened. Our spiritual understanding will be expanded by what we see there.

JOHN THE BAPTIST

I saw John the Baptist standing in Heaven's opening. Although I didn't interact with him, I could see him preaching. It seemed as if he were still on the earth, expressing the heart of John 3:30: "He must become greater; I must become less." John preached about those who are humble, the lowly ones. He proclaimed loudly:

> "God is going to take the ones who have lowered themselves and who do not even appear on the maps of human plans, and He is going to put them in the center of Kingdom activity."

God is going to use the foolish things—humble men and women of this world who have great equity with His heart in Heaven—to displace and nullify those things that are in the established order of the world system. God is inviting us to pay such an awesome price so that He can place us in the very center of the world and inherit all that belongs to Him.

> But God chose the foolish things of the world to shame the wise; God chose the weak things of the world to shame the strong. He chose the lowly things of this world and the despised things—and the things that are not—to nullify the things that are, so that no one may boast before him.
> —1 CORINTHIANS 1:27–29

Throughout history, God has raised up many unlikely individuals to accomplish His work; He has not changed His ways today. He is not looking for those already in authority; He does not need man to approve His choices.

Individuals who long for celebrities to get saved just so these famous, influential people can minister are deceived about how God wants to work in our generation. Others hope that wealthy business owners get saved so they will give away their wealth. However, those who think this way are completely misguided about how God works.

In the days ahead, the Holy Spirit will use many who come in the imminent harvest, but God also longs to use many believers who are currently in fellowship with His divine purposes and equip *them* to invade the very heart of industries on earth, displaying the creative power of God.

God showed me that many in the Church who selfishly want celebrities to be redeemed do not understand His ways. Such individuals pray for Britney Spears to get saved so this sensuous rock star will serve as a godly role model for their children. But the principle behind these self-seeking desires can be found in Proverbs:

> The wicked desire the plunder of evil men,
> but the root of the righteous flourishes.
>
> —PROVERBS 12:12

God longs to bring to the forefront His hidden ones— individuals who are rooted and grounded in divine love. He wants to create wealth through them. God doesn't need the wealth of the rich or the favor of kings to accomplish His eternal purposes. God loves to move through the weak and lowly.

Believers who are firmly planted in God's love don't desire to plunder the unrighteous, nor do they covet the abilities and talents that some celebrities have prostituted to acquire wealth. Rather, they long for the world's riches so that Jesus' inheritance may be granted to Him. The desire for worldly wealth is purified when we desire Heaven's creative spirit to birth a fresh Kingdom manifestation on earth, and we do not seek to imitate any worldly industry or position.

God does not wish to bring the present Judeo-Christian culture to human industries. He actually wants to bring a counterculture to those industries—a new model patterned after a higher spiritual value system. This heavenly pattern shall invade the world!

SPIRITUAL FRUIT

When John the Baptist had finished his sermon, he disappeared. As I continued to gaze into the Heavens, I saw many treasures stored up for the Righteous One. Treasure existed of every type, and it was all for Jesus. It was on display.

As I looked into Heaven, I realized I was seeing into the age to come. It was as if Jesus had already had His entire purpose fulfilled and He had returned. Suddenly, I was standing in some sort of treasury room in Heaven, where resources that had been used on earth were invested into our eternal inheritance.

Then, these treasures became a grapevine, and I was looking over a luscious vineyard in Heaven. I knew that these treasures and resources were eternal fruit. They were a vineyard that produced the new wine of communion between Jesus and His bride. Each resource on earth that had been invested into the purpose of Jesus grew spiritual fruit for us in Heaven. This fruit helped bond us to our testimony of love for Jesus.

APOSTOLIC FINANCES

Standing in Heaven, I began to hear a divine, precious melody that could not ever be adequately described by human means. An angel was singing in the most vibrant, clear pitch. Here is an inadequate rendition of his song:

"These are apostolic finances;
What they have built can never be torn.
Though the natural will fade,
The fruit will remain for all eternity.
We will drink the heavenly wine of communion
Produced from the fruit of our testimony of righteous
    acts on earth.
We were made for so much more than we ever realized.
He is just and repays all our sacrifice, all our obedience,
With His gracious love.
His mercy endures forever!"

This song and the lovely fragrance filling the atmosphere permeated my spirit.

A HEAVENLY MAKEOVER

As I marveled at these things, the Minister of Finance appeared from a portal in Heaven and flew past me. I considered following him, but instead, I just watched where he went. He was earthbound.

He stopped in the room of a businessman, inviting that man into a heavenly experience much like I was in. I watched this businessman receive his eternal calling; it was imparted into his mind, spirit, and emotions, and he became eternally clothed with divine purpose. Angels arrived from the four corners of Heaven and began to give him a heavenly makeover.

Cosmetic surgeons could not have done what happened to this man's spirit. He was transformed by God's glory as he was prepared to take on his bridal purpose, as described in Revelation 19:5–8, where the bride adorned herself with fine linens that represented the righteous acts of the saints.

Angels were sent to help prepare this businessman to pay the price of obedience for partnering with Heaven through righteous acts. Such a flurry of activity was happening in and around him that I could barely see him for a few moments. I began to think of Paul, who wrote about a "longing to be clothed" in eternal glory (2 Corinthians 5:1–5). I understood that while we yearn to be clothed with our heavenly dwelling, we are nonetheless clothed, even if only by faith.

After the angels had added the finishing touches to this man, they stepped back, and a heavenly light poured down on the man from a higher place in Heaven. Amazingly, he now resembled the angelic Minister of Finance himself! How awesomely God had adorned him to resemble the angels, who reflect the finest attributes of God Himself. This man was not only partnering with Heaven through his business, but he was taking on God's virtue and attributes for this very partnership. He was emulating the divine order of Heaven!

Suddenly, I saw many others undergoing the same kind of preparation. People began to receive money and resources just as I had seen in earlier visions. This time, however, the people who received money were actually assuming the appearance of the resource angels who worked for the Minister of Finance. A few, like the businessman I just described, even looked like the Minister of Finance himself. What an honored position among humans to look like the heavenly hosts, who resemble Jesus.

I emerged from this vision with the strange sensation of the keys embedded in my chest. I could still feel the cold metal inside me.

CHAPTER FIVE

SECOND
VISITATION

"I walk in the way of righteousness,
along the paths of justice,
bestowing wealth on those who love me
and making their treasuries full."

—PROVERBS 8:20–21

On August 20, 2002, I was on a much-needed ministry break, staying with some friends at their lake home in Wisconsin. Early one morning, before sunrise, I was caught up in a vision and encountered the Minister of Finance once again. Before I could respond or react, he spoke:

"The Lord, the Lord has commissioned us on the earth for a work to sow sovereign monies, to effect projects that will bring forth the beauty of Jesus upon the earth. You are to proclaim the word of the Lord."

As it was in his first visitation, the Minister of Finance's voice was like a trumpet heralding much melody. It also carried a strange pitch that went straight into my spirit. His message was like listening to a song. I was reminded that this angel had been given authority to release finances for projects and industries that God had already injected into human hearts.

RELATIONAL NETWORKS

Then I entered another vision where I saw large nets spanning geographical areas. Each net originated from individual points of light representing a believer or a company of believers in the secular arena who had been called forth into a greater purpose.

Links between the lights were purposed, relational connections. Some links represented established friendships that would now engage divine purpose. Other links were being drawn as I watched; tens of thousands of lines were delineated in only a few minutes.

What I saw reminded me of Isaiah's prophecy of dramatic changes happening in short lengths of time:

> "Before she goes into labor,
> she gives birth;
> before the pains come upon her,
> she delivers a son.
> Who has ever heard of such a thing?
> Who has ever seen such things?
> Can a country be born in a day
> or a nation be brought forth in a moment?
> Yet no sooner is Zion in labor
> than she gives birth to her children.
>
> —ISAIAH 66:7–8

God is about to birth His government across the earth in a surprisingly short season. This sudden appearing will serve as one of the demonstrations of His Kingdom's supernatural nature, which God wants to display to confound the wisdom of the wise.

In these networks of people—represented by white lines—I saw doors of future opportunities being created for individuals who were faithful to divine appointments and purposeful connections.

At some point, I believe God will begin to harvest entire networks of relationships, making them divine nets of provision and purpose. The net I saw was a tool to capture thousands upon thousands of hearts with God's passion.

Many people have been on spiritual journeys that connect them across the map by divine appointment and for divine purposes. In this vision, I was seeing how angels assigned to this sphere were helping bring forth this desired outcome.

When the angels of resource connected one person (or group) to another, the Minister of Finance began planting the gold of Jesus over different people's heads. Jesus' gold would hover over people who had no idea it was there. As these individuals reached up with their intercession for God's will in Heaven to be made real on the earth, the gold would descend on them. It seemed as if they had received a "breaker anointing," a breakthrough from Heaven itself, causing them to receive in the natural realm a manifestation of what was planted over them in the spiritual realm. The hands of their faith reached above their heads and captured these divine resources.

Right now, so many people are pregnant with God's purposes, and they don't even know it. The Western world is presently experiencing a divine frustration that is parabolically like a woman in her last month waiting to give birth. We need to remember that God is so faithful to deliver the fruit of our womb:

> "Do I bring to the moment of birth
> and not give delivery?" says the LORD.
> "Do I close up the womb
> when I bring to delivery?" says your God.
>
> —ISAIAH 66:9

God will birth everything He has conceived in our spiritual being. He is faithful.

We are approaching the season when this birthing will happen with such a sudden anointing that it may take the world by surprise. This process will hit a token few very soon and keep unfolding until we cry out as an entire generation.

> The LORD has made proclamation
> to the ends of the earth:
> "Say to the Daughter of Zion
> 'See, your Savior comes!
> See, his reward is with him,
> and his recompense accompanies him.'"
>
> —ISAIAH 62:11

SENT WITH A NOBLE PURPOSE

As the Minister of Finance was talking to me, he began to explain that for Jesus to inherit the world in one generation, people are going to be sent with Kingdom purpose into every aspect and culture of the earth. He explained:

"God's plan is to use people in business, the Internet, multimedia, entertainment, politics, education, medical fields, environment, science, music, and the military; those lowly ones who carry the purpose of God will infiltrate virtually every type of human activity.

"The fivefold ministry is for every area and arena of the world where those who follow the Lord dwell. It is not limited to humanly devised structures, but goes wherever the Spirit inhabits. The fruit of fivefold ministry is eternal, and fivefold government transcends much of the earthly mind-set His bride expects and believes it to be."

The Minister of Finance talked about the bride with such affection. He wasn't rebuking us, nor did he sound offended. Rather, he was excited about the heavenly revelation about to unfold, bringing the bride into her eternal purpose.

Then the Minister of Finance touched my head, and I understood that apostolic leaders will be in the entertainment industry, evangelistic leaders in politics, pastoral leaders in education, prophetic ministers in science, teachers in the arts, etc. In other words, Kingdom-building roles are not limited to the traditional form of Western-world church, but they will also build the Kingdom of God in every aspect of society.

If an apostle is one who builds the Kingdom of God by helping govern and administrate the Spirit's activity on earth, why would we limit this role to ministerial positions within the walls of traditional congregations? An example of an apostolic builder in a nontraditional ministerial position is a friend who has an apostolic calling and is beginning to build Kingdom values into the entertainment industry. He is supporting young movie production houses with both vision and finances, planting them in Hollywood with prayer, biblical studies, and evangelism. He is fathering a generation of entertainers who are about to come forth. With signs, wonders, and a father's heart, he is building Kingdom mandates into places of business—they have become his congregations. The Kingdom is spreading like fire.

The highest call for all who know the Lord is to deliver to Jesus everything that belongs to Him. It is *not* limited to spending time in religious activities sponsored by ministries and organizations; although these are valuable, we need to have an equal value for callings in any arena. This entails building God's temple amid every people, nation, tribe, and tongue, spreading God's dominion everywhere we have the opportunity.

FIVEFOLD MINISTRY AND THE NEW WINESKIN

I then saw brand-new baby skin that resembled a huge pelt. I knew this was a picture of the new wineskin (Matthew 9:17). It was a living skin, fresh and pink, made up of people instead of dead, dry structures.

New wineskins for the Body of Christ will be birthed from this revolutionary understanding of the fivefold ministry. This new wineskin will begin to manifest in full authority in secular arenas, which will catalyze an expansion of the Kingdom unlike anything we have ever seen.

The presently vast, entrenched dividing walls between secular and ministerial operations in the Church will shift into a synergistic flow between the two. Each will become dependent upon the other in the way it is supposed to be. The angel continued:

"Those in secular positions of business and finance are not the counterparts to those in ministry positions. They are not to be married, taking on two identities to become one, but they are one and the same already. Jesus is their counterpart. They are to be one and then married to Him."

The angel was describing an elusive truth. As he spoke, I understood how confusion has run rampant in the Church with regard to secular and ministry roles being separate. Some leaders, following the "king and priest" theology, have sought to build unity between the two by emphasizing the differences of the roles. They've related ministry to priestly activities and secular careers to kingly activities, and in this way, perhaps the two would seem to be more dependent on each other. This has a kernel of truth in it, yet this teaching can be divisive and delegate too much control to one or the other.

The Minister of Finance was clear when he said that Heaven looks at human roles as equal parts of the same body; we are not to think that we are married together—we are already one body. Together, we are being prepared to marry Jesus.

THE HEBREW MIND-SET

Believers tend to struggle with integrating their life functions. Typically, we don't know how to flow in all areas of life from the same Kingdom mind-set. If our identity in our secular job is inconsistent with our ministry for God, we then fragment in the ways we approach daily activities in each sphere. By compartmentalizing our lives, we will not be flowing out of our spiritual core, which is dependent on Him.

God endowed the Hebrew culture with such complete

truths about how to function without separating from oneself or other members of one's community. The Hebrew mind-set did not compartmentalize or separate one area of life from another. In fact, it taught—and in some Jewish circles still teaches—the most holistic way of living, where everything in life is connected and flows together.

On the other hand, the Greek mind-set, which is what the entire Western world has adopted, actually causes one to engage in discrete modes of operation for each different activity. It is not simply a different means of processing and thinking than the Hebrew mind-set, but it actually contradicts the way, truth, and life that God intended us to act, think, and live.

In the Greek mind-set, people often take on a different "personality" for talking on the telephone than when talking to their children. Or they might have a strategic mind-set for business, but they don't know how to access that same strategy for their family relationships.

In Hebrew culture, however, one learns a set of principles and applies them in all the venues of life, not dispersing them for different functions and relationships. Thus, biblical studies have an added measure of importance because they train us in Hebrew mindedness.

Before this expansion of a heavenly mind-set can happen in the natural arena, however, individuals must receive an expansion in their spirit so they can integrate God's noble purposes. 1 Corinthians 2:16 states that we can have the "mind of Christ." God is looking for people who would rid themselves of the common Greek mind-set. His desire is that we become whole so we may attain our high calling by aligning our hearts with His noble purposes.

Paul instructs Timothy to be a divine instrument:

In a large house there are articles not only of gold and silver, but also of wood and clay; some are for noble purposes and some for ignoble. If a man cleanses himself from the latter, he will be an instrument for noble purposes, made holy, useful to the Master and prepared to do any good work.

—2 TIMOTHY 2:20–21

PERSONAL TOKENS BEING RELEASED

I emerged from this second visitation, and the corresponding visions, totally undone. I couldn't even tell my friends what had happened. Little did I know that God was about to give me a personal testimony of His intentions, releasing divine resources in my life. I was about to walk out a prophetic parable of what I had glimpsed in the spirit realm.

Without knowing about my visionary encounter, my friends had heard from God clearly that morning: They were supposed to buy me a new car for my ministry because my old car was dying. They went to great measures to secretly find out exactly what kind of car I wanted so they could surprise me with it.

When they delivered the car to me, it was so profound, not just because it was an extravagant provision, but because it was a token. To me, cars represent the epitome of our spiritual quest—the prophetic role destiny plays through us in our journey of life. Cars are a metaphor for our calling, how our spirit moves in God. So in prophetic language, cars often represent ministries or occupations, and I knew this "picture" indicated a higher ministry or occupation God wanted me to embrace.

I also knew that this was coming at the end of a long season in which God had been conforming me to His image,

His plans, and His character. I was dying to myself, painfully sacrificing my own agenda so that I could lay hold of Heaven's. In no way had I arrived at spiritual perfection, but this token was released at the end of the long, hard season as a picture of what was to come in my relationship with God. I knew there was a price to walking in the anointing—but it would be worth it. Even as I received this token, I knew the future prize of cooperating with Jesus' intimate friendship would be worth all trials and suffering.

As I pondered what God was saying to me, I discerned two messages:

1. God will supply His people with "new vehicles"—in other words, a renewing or new installment of spiritual calling to secure their hearts' desires—but He will do this through the Spirit of Power.
2. God will release tokens from Heaven that will affect us in very personal ways as we partner with God. These tokens go beyond mere provisions; they help to advance the very Kingdom dynamics mentioned in this book.

The Holy Spirit reminded me of the commission given to the overcomers in the church of Thyatira:

"To him who overcomes and does my will to the end, I will give authority over the nations."

—REVELATION 2:26

If we overcome the spirit of the world in whatever occupation we choose, God will give us dominion and power—a new means to operate in a higher role than that available in the natural. God is placing those who come into agreement with Heaven in roles of authority far surpassing what any mere human can give. Just as Paul observed in Ephesians 1 and 2, it is important to understand this authority so that we can overcome the dynamics of striving to achieve it, even in the midst of secular occupations.

POSTURE OF HUMILITY

To qualify for the lofty purpose of partnering with God, there is a process we must undergo. It doesn't matter whether you already have solid leadership experience and resources, or if you are just beginning the "promise journey." A price must be paid before God will give you Kingdom authority (a means for your faith) to walk out, thus spreading the investment to bring forth the treasured ones of God.

Many in our culture today are called to produce wealth through the Spirit of Might. During my visitation from the Minister of Finance, he opened a Bible and pointed at a Scripture in the Old Testament that expanded my understanding of this:

> You may say to yourself, "My power and the strength of my hands have produced this wealth for me." But remember the LORD your God, for it is he who gives you the ability to produce wealth, and so confirms his covenant, which he swore to your forefathers, as it is today.
>
> —DEUTERONOMY 8:17–18

The Western world has a plague of pride. We have been allotted abundant grace to prosper. Especially in the United States, a supernatural flow of riches is in the land. We have natural resources, coupled with prestigious intellectual and creative blessings, which have led to innumerable inventions and wealth.

Many even in the Body of Christ have not recognized this grace. They believe their own strength has produced these riches. But our hands are not capable of doing so without divine grace. Believers have even written books and preached sermons that give detailed models of their strategic accomplishments, but these often depreciate God's supernatural love and provision that qualified their endeavors.

Consider what it might look like if we were without this divine grace in the Western world. We would probably become like many third world countries held hostage in poverty and hunger. Perhaps it would take time for our economic structures to collapse, but it would become obvious to everyone that we had been divinely blessed and that this blessing was no longer available. This is why it is so important for us—especially individuals in the secular arena—to humble ourselves.

It is exciting to hear that God has given us—through His covenant—the ability to produce wealth. Now more than ever, I believe that this is true, and if we can align ourselves with the covenant purpose of that wealth, then we will be able to make quick advances that will baffle the world.

NOT BY MIGHT NOR POWER

"'Not by might nor by power, but by My Spirit,' says the Lord Almighty" (Zechariah 4:6). This was addressed to Zerubbabel, the governor of Judah who was called to rebuild God's temple. Zerubbabel was forbidden to trust in human resources to accomplish the task. Instead, he was dependent on God for the financial and labor provisions for this undertaking.

Zechariah 4:6 has become a cliché in Christian circles. Many are unaware that it deals with a warning in Deuteronomy 8:17:

> You may say to yourself, "My power and the strength of my hands have produced this wealth for me."

It may surprise you, but these two Scriptures are married; Zechariah's challenge referred to Moses' warning in Deuteronomy to always remember that God is our Source of life. This realization is pivotal to us today, because we must comprehend that we are dependent solely on anointing, which originates from God's desire to provide where He leads.

Even in the natural realm, everything comes from the Creator. The enemy can only manipulate, control, or counterfeit things of God by seducing humans into rebellion. The enemy cannot create wealth or ignite strategies to attract new wealth. He can only manipulate humanity to compromise and influence the heart of wickedness that dwells in men and women, thereby perverting the creative spirit. As James understood:

> Every good and perfect gift is from above, coming down from the Father of the heavenly lights, who does not change like shifting shadows.
>
> —JAMES 1:17

Before we were born, God considered us. Before we needed to be redeemed, God began to plan our existence— the gifts and talents He would bestow on us. He formed in us the ability to create in the natural realm based on the inspiration the Spirit placed in our nature. God never changed His mind regarding anyone He created on earth. He still releases the abilities He had planned for each of us, because it was part of His plan and nature to create us in His image (Genesis 1:26). Paul understood this when he wrote:

> God's gifts and his call are irrevocable. Just as you who were at one time disobedient to God have now received mercy as a result of their disobedience, so they too have now become disobedient in order that they too may now receive mercy as a result of God's mercy to you. For God has bound all men over to disobedience so that he may have mercy on them all.
>
> Oh, the depth of the riches of the wisdom and
> knowledge of God!
> How unsearchable his judgments,
> and his paths beyond tracing out!
> —ROMANS 11:29–33

I believe Paul is stating that God will use His people to show mercy to the world, even while those in the world have used their gifts for lesser purposes than giving Jesus what is His and becoming allies of Heaven. As people walk out their giftings and callings on earth with the agenda of Heaven as their focus, the whole world comes under significant spiritual blessing. This is one of the ways God's mercy is shown to unbelievers.

It is not in God's nature to control us, so if we begin to work in a lesser way than we were designed to, He can only invite us into a higher place. If we do not respond to God when He draws us, then we become stumbling blocks because of our own self-centered desires. Even good Christian people can become the enemies of what God wants to accomplish: If their agenda and will do not imitate His, then they are against His. This is why it is so important to let our spirit and understanding be disciplined by God's Word so that we can comprehend His desires and will.

The main reason our desires do not match those of Heaven is that we are motivated by materialism and pride, which Satan loves to play off of and manipulate. We may then use the very attributes God has given us to gain a selfish status that is counterproductive.

In the Bible, Job and the prophets ask God a question that He takes exquisite care in answering: "Why do the wicked prosper?" In essence, there are many answers, but they all boil down to one common denominator: The wicked prosper because God will not control human nature. He will only invite us into His affections.

God is looking at the panorama of eternity. He is not threatened when humanity steps in His way. He gave us free will, for better or for worse. He is all-knowing and can maneuver around or break through any human dynamic in ways we do not understand.

The disobedient are prospering now only in a very limited earthly economy. God, however, calls us to live in a much higher economy—that of Heaven. Once you begin to prosper in Heaven's money management program, you will never covet earthly prosperity again. You will never claim justice by entreating God for your natural provisions to meet your earthly needs. Instead, you will long for even more Kingdom provision, which not only satisfies earthly needs but also goes far beyond—linking you to the heartbeat of Heaven.

CHAPTER SIX

THE ECONOMY OF HEAVEN

The LORD will send a blessing on your barns and on everything you put your hand to. The LORD your God will bless you in the land he is giving you.

—DEUTERONOMY 28:8

I n 1997, I had a supernatural experience that dramatically marked my life. I was transported to a heavenly realm and taken to a huge warehouse. It was so vast that I could not find the room's perimeters—I could not distinguish the ceiling or walls—even though the room was enclosed. Never have I seen a structure so immense. It reminded me of how much space there is in the eternal heart of God.

An angel who oversaw the storehouse was assigned to show me around. As he took me on a tour through different sections of the building, I was gripped by anticipation.

"What is this place?" I asked.

His eyes lit up. He smiled and replied, "This is the storehouse of Heaven. Every provision that will ever be needed in this age for Jesus to receive the fullness of His inheritance is here, ready and waiting for those who would partner with Him and would call it forth."

I was stunned. The revelation of this abundant and pre-planned provision was too much for me to comprehend. Not only did God the Father know us before we were even in our mothers' wombs, but He designed a comprehensive plan of provision that would last until His Son returns. I was transfixed by the awe of God, by how He literally has created provision for us that is so real, all we need to do is access it. No wonder Jesus taught us to ask the Father to manifest everything we need on earth as it is in Heaven! It really exists there now!

The angel and I strolled through Heaven's storehouse for a long time, looking at the many types of provisions. I will mention a few of the areas shown to me, just to build your perspective of what is available to us. I hope as you read this that God begins to instill a desire within your heart to survey the storehouse for yourself.

THE DEPARTMENT OF CREATIVE MIRACLES

The angel and I walked down aisles of glory. It was unlike any place I had ever been. My mind almost hurt just trying to take in all the awesome landscapes. Eventually, we reached a room within the larger warehouse that reminded me of a trade show I had been to once.

The aisles in this room were so large that I cannot describe all that I saw. One section was dedicated to the physical body. Aisle upon aisle displayed body parts of every type. I walked down an aisle and found a leg. It was one of tens of thousands of legs lining a rack that almost reminded me of something you'd find in a meat factory, in some odd way.

The leg I noticed had a toe tag. But then I realized all the legs on the aisle had tags. The specific tag I read bore a woman's name and had the date it would be delivered. This woman on earth would literally be restored to walking one day! Can you imagine that God has already made provision for various limbs and all we need is the faith to manifest it?

I looked at my angelic companion and asked, "What is this room?" I felt like weeping.

"This is the Department of Creative Miracles," he responded.

He didn't need to explain it further. Surrounding me were eyeballs, ears, teeth, hair, toes, fingers, bones, muscles, organs—so many body parts! And these body parts constituted only one section of the Creative Miracles Department. There were many other kinds of creative miracles as well.

HEAVENLY MANNA

A section away, I noticed angels preparing food. Every type of meat healthful for human consumption filled the table. A vast quantity of breads, oats, milk, clean water, and vegetables had been accumulated. A grand preparation was going on, and I immediately thought of the wedding supper of the Lamb in Revelation 19:9.

"I know what you are thinking, but the foods here are not for His banquet," the angel said. "These foods will be called forth and given through miraculous provision and multiplication for the poor of the earth and the poor in spirit."

Instantly, I was overwhelmed. The angel also explained that an entire section was reserved just for animal food. This made sense, especially for people who lived in persecuted countries who might not be able to feed their families, let alone their livestock or pets. God has provision even for the animals we have dominion over!

All this provision is obviously something we are going to have to exercise great faith for in the world. We will see miraculous provision in countries and people groups who need it most. There will be manifestations on a more visible level that will demonstrate, especially to the poor, that God is a supernatural God of love. There are a few reports throughout history of the multiplication or supernatural provision of food, mostly in third world nations.

I know that Iris Ministries in Mozambique, Africa, has experienced this phenomenon many times, as have our dear friends at Global Children's Ministries; they have seen the multiplication not only of food but clothing as well. I asked them why they thought God had granted this miracle to them when there are so many dying of hunger every day. The sentiment they shared was that they were dependent on God to manifest His blessing supernaturally because of the desperate needs of the people. They were not building with a humanitarian effort alone but in such a way that puts a demand on Heaven's response.

We continued walking, and I followed my angelic friend past the diverse, awesome delicacies into another section that dwarfed the others.

A SUPERNATURAL FAITH DIMENSION

We found ourselves walking toward a cloud of color and light that resembled pictures captured by the Hubble Telescope. The angel invited me to walk into the cloud. When I did, I found myself in the middle of magnificent light. It was as if I had stepped into the Father's heart. Light shot inside me, empowering me with creative faith.

This was the place in God's heart everyone longs to see.

It was a faith realm that in many ways is hard to describe. While in this realm, I could believe for any creative miracle of provision that would equip a person for his or her destiny.

Other people were in the cloud; they seemed to be praying on earth, somehow accessing this place in God's heart. As they prayed in agreement with what was available in Heaven, the limited natural realm expanded to admit the miraculous power of God.

In this place, I felt I could ask God for anything— money, creative miracles, mountains to move, anything! Then as quickly as I had entered this cloud, I was back in the storehouse on the other side.

I looked at my angelic friend with amazement. He had not traveled into the cloud with me. "That is a place in the Father's heart reserved for humans," he explained. I realized that God had designed us to commune with His heart in a way that even the angels could not.

ROOMS OF DIVINE ARCHITECTURE

Next, we were transported to a different area in the storehouse. "Welcome to the rooms of Divine Architecture," announced my angelic companion.

Miniature models of buildings were everywhere. I saw materials that were fully prepared for architectural works and new types of structures and buildings that had been assembled to withstand global calamities.

As we passed by these miniature edifices, I saw entire city blocks with new demographic plans from Heaven. When I looked more closely, I realized these blocks were living and breathing with people and traffic flowing through them; they seemed to already exist in finished forms. God's plans are *this* complete, needing only our agreement in order to manifest in our generation.

Circular tables were overlaid with plans and blueprints for various kinds of buildings that would be built to glorify God: stadiums, places of worship, businesses, schools, and hospitals.

While some building projects were brand new, another section held remodeling plans for current hospitals, schools, stadiums, banks, political buildings, offices, businesses, amusement parks, theaters, film studios, and a host of other types of buildings. God had lists and lists of buildings He intended to direct for Kingdom purposes. I couldn't believe how many things God desires to own that currently exist now on earth.

Each plan had a seal on it. Some of the seals had names and dates; others just had names, while some were left unmarked, waiting for whomever would commit to that plan to bring forth the name as well as the purpose of Jesus. What an opportunity and occupation to be an architect with access to Heaven's divine architecture!

THE CREATIVE INVENTIONS SECTION

After this, we were quickly carried away by the Spirit to a different section called Creative Inventions. Although it was a vast area, it seemed that each place we entered became larger. Lights and colors swirled around, and the Holy Spirit seemed to hover and flash like lightning. Somehow I knew the Holy Spirit had visited many people in their minds and imaginations with the same flashes that I was witnessing in Heaven. He would spark the capacity to invent and create what I was viewing in this storehouse.

Every type of technology was represented here: agricultural, computer science, medical. Many cures for diseases were in this section. Toys were here, sound devices, video and multimedia machines—so many basic materials already known to humanity that could be combined in new configurations to create revolutionary advancements for the earth. The Spirit of Revelation would have to reveal the various combinations.

Angels guarded certain inventions. I tried to discern why guards existed in this area, then I noticed some people trying to gain illegal access through witchcraft to steal these inventions. I was incredulous that the enemy was so bold, yet as I watched one invention, I began to understand why.

In a vision, I saw God send an angel to earth and offer a Christian the invitation to steward an invention. The man began to create the invention, but he ran into trouble with his finances and relationships because of the warfare surrounding the project. Instead of interceding and beseeching God for provision and protection, the man remained immersed in his work and closed his heart to Heaven.

During this time, a very wealthy man was sent by a demonic force to meet this Christian. The wealthy man offered to fund the man's invention. The Christian peremptorily agreed to this, but later when they sealed the deal, the wealthy man stole the technology since he had manipulated the business deal in his favor. Because he had lost faith in Heaven's provision and God's faithfulness, the Christian had been so desperate and rash that he would have said yes to almost any contract. So the enemy stole and won the use of a precious, divinely inspired communication system, which Satan has used to defile humanity all over the globe with every form of perversion. After this, I understood why guardians watched over this and other areas of the heavenly storehouse.

The same creative Spirit inventing science was also inventing the arts. In the same section, I was guided through rooms and rooms that were specifically dedicated to the creative arts. A book would be required to describe this arts section. Because there is coming such an astounding release of Heaven's arts upon the earth, creative arts centers will pop up in cities around the world, redefining the boundaries between the different artistic media and their expression and housing many artistic forms of expression in a single building.

HEAVEN'S MUSIC STOREROOM

At the edge of the creative arts section was a fourth section—Heaven's Music Storeroom. It was in full use.

The music arts section was especially interesting because it overlapped the very throne room of Heaven. So many instruments were being played and so many songs were being sung that it would have seemed chaotic, but my spirit was able to sample comfortably a variety of different styles and genres. Sounds that had not yet been created, accompanied by modified and even brand-new instruments, were rampant. Songbooks full of new expressions had been written to unlock hearts and woo them to a deeper intimacy with God. The number of songbooks seemed infinite, and all of them pleased God immensely—the only One who would ever be able to count the reams upon reams of songs still to be written for Him. King Solomon had touched this creative realm; he is reputed to have written more than a thousand songs in his lifetime that glorified God. Imagine when an entire generation taps into this celestial sphere!

Angels who were playing songs composed by the Holy Spirit in the throne room were able to go down to earth and impart these songs to others. In some cases, they would bring people to Heaven to listen to the indescribable sounds created fresh in the atmosphere of this awesome place.

I also noticed that demons would appear and try to plagiarize and steal these heavenly sounds and songs. They could endure the atmosphere for only a few seconds, but they would still try to simulate what they had heard and give their horrendous renditions to people on earth, who would subsequently twist and pervert them to offend God. This was Satan's preemptive strike on the music industries God desired to inspire.

Heavenly guard angels, however, armed with something like giant fly swatters, would search for demonic intruders. They would squelch the enemies who were trying to steal a peek or listen in on the music arts section. These demonic attempts could do nothing to thwart the mighty celestial music slated for release on earth. Satanic extortions were ineffective in permanently damaging God's Kingdom.

A PICTURE OF HEAVEN'S ECONOMY

We walked through other sections of the storehouse; many we bypassed, but I could see they were available. Shelves of books could be written about them. I will name a few to whet your imagination:

- A garment section for cloths that would reflect Heaven;
- A farming section to inherit divine strategies on how to feed the earth and steward food;
- An educational section with creative teaching for students young and old;
- A prophetic section with multifarious revelations just waiting to be birthed on earth;

• And so many more!

Toward the end of my tour, the angel in charge of the storehouse told me, "This storehouse is a picture, or a metaphor or type, of how Heaven's economy operates."

As I have written previously, my heart was filled with the understanding that everything we need to bring Jesus His full reward has already been prepared by the Father. He will hold nothing back! The Father has carefully created these provisions in the spirit realm of Heaven. They only need to be recognized and then apprehended by those who have eyes to see—anyone who chooses to partner with God.

Jesus is in Heaven interceding for us. He is praying for our spiritual eyes to be opened to see everything that awaits us as His recompense. Can you envision Jesus seated at the right hand of the Father, surveying the earth and the ones He loves? He is aware of what is available to us, and He is pouring out petition and prayer for us regarding every opportunity, every resource, every spiritual manifestation offered as an investment. Angelic armies wait to assist Him in commissioning human warriors to extend His Kingdom. This is what constitutes the economy of Heaven.

I believe the prophet Joel saw this economy being released on the earth when he prophesied:

"And afterward,
I will pour out my Spirit on all people.
Your sons and daughters will prophesy,
your old men will dream dreams,
your young men will see visions.
Even on my servants, both men and women,
I will pour out my Spirit in those days.

I will show wonders in the heavens
and on the earth,
blood and fire and billows of smoke."

—JOEL 2:28–30

God shall release an entire generation of people who live by His Spirit and love the object of the Father's desire—His Son. We shall behold wonders in Heaven and shall call them forth to attest to God's glory on earth. We shall start to move in the creative power of the Holy Spirit, imitating God:

. . . the God who gives life to the dead and calls
things that are not as though they were.

—ROMANS 4:17

When we know the reality of God's desire and when we experience more of the fullness of Him in our lives, we can begin to move in His authority, calling forth everything to bear witness with full power on earth as it is in Heaven. Because Jesus understood this dimension of unity, He instructed us to pray and expect to see results.

When He walked the earth, Jesus walked in absolute unity with the agenda of the Father. He prayed, fasted, and studied the Scripture—all to understand the heart of His Father so that He could demonstrate that heart to the earth. He entered a union with the Father that wasn't based on knowledge only; it was a spiritual bond that allowed Him to anticipate the Father's desires. He instructed us to pray out of this same union and expect to see results. But to move with this kind of authority, we must first encounter His desire. We must operate in unity with His heart. A storehouse full of resources awaits those who live connected to the Father's heart. This is God's economy—to call forth what is not as though it were!

You see, Jesus is a desperate man. He's not impatient or unknowing . . . just desperate. His Father promised Him a world as His inheritance (Psalm 2:8; John 3:16), and therefore, His desire will remain unsatisfied until that inheritance is fully released.

The Father promised Jesus two things:

1. Many throughout all human generations would enter the Kingdom of God.
2. At the climax, one generation would cry out for the fullness of God's plan to manifest on earth.

God promised that the bride of Christ would cry out passionately—in agreement with the Holy Spirit—for Jesus to rend the Heavens and to come down in the fullness of His destiny and glean His reward.

The Spirit and the bride say, "Come!"

—REVELATION 22:17

HEAVEN'S BURNING DESIRE

All Heaven shares Jesus' desperation. Thus, all Heaven is dedicated to Jesus' purpose. The Father has delegated Heaven to worship His Son and by this worship also to serve this same purpose. Therefore, an economy is released in Heaven that is unified in stewardship and partnership with Jesus' high calling for all that belongs to Him to be brought forth. Angels delight in this economy, and we can partake of the same joy in fellowship with Heaven's purpose.

God will never release authority for a natural kingdom to be built in Jesus' name if it doesn't have a higher focus on the purpose of eternity. In other words, if any natural endeavor doesn't seek to reflect Jesus and the glory that is due Him, then it does not belong to Him. God will not release anything from His storehouse that does not grow eternal fruit. Therefore, any undertaking must not have its beginning and end on earth or it will belong to the earth. Godly treasure must be stored up in Heaven.

Jesus never desired any worldly thing while He was on earth unless it had a Kingdom fulfillment. So surely He will not desire worldly things now that He is seated beside the Father in Heaven. He did not desire human authority or dominion on earth, because something greater burned in His heart. He knew He must remain in union with Heaven and that, later, all authority, power, and dominion would belong to Him, in addition to every title of authority that already belonged to Him:

> . . . which [the Father] exerted in Christ when he
> raised him from the dead and seated him at his right
> hand in the heavenly realms, far above all rule and
> authority, power and dominion, and every title that
> can be given, not only in the present age but also in
> the one to come. And God placed all things under
> his feet and appointed him to be head over every-
> thing for the church, which is his body, the fullness of
> him who fills everything in every way.
> —EPHESIANS 1:20–23

No human authority can be given to align our heart with

Jesus' heart. This authority comes only from the Father.

Human beings often strive to gain and wield authority. They form human networks; they are focused on pleasing others, gaining positions—serving themselves, getting absorbed in politics, dominating others. This describes the human culture, the earthly economy.

Jesus, on the other hand, always demonstrated a different way of life. He showed that love wields the greatest authority and can displace any authority gained by human effort. Jesus created a new economy whose currency is spiritual hunger. An appetite not just for the trappings of Heaven but for its very core—hunger for Jesus!

CHAPTER SEVEN

THE JUSTICE OF HEAVEN

"Rise and thresh, O Daughter of Zion,
for I will give you horns of iron;
I will give you hoofs of bronze
and you will break to pieces many nations."
You will devote their ill-gotten gains to the LORD,
their wealth to the Lord of all the earth.

—MICAH 4:13

One of the most profound—and often the most mis-understood—principles in the Bible is justice. Heaven's justice system is nothing like that of the world. As a matter of fact, justice throughout the world is one of the main targets of demonic abuse. If the enemy can destroy the justice system of a nation, he can crush hope and faith in human hearts and perpetrate every manner of evil.

Righteous justice is demonstrated hundreds of times throughout the Bible, yet the men and women who read Scripture often conflict with it the most. The good news is that justice is so precious to God's heart. It is one of the main con-duits through which Heaven's economy will manifest in the days to come. Even as God pours out His temporal judgments stated in the Bible, His covenant people will steward His compassion and the heavenly resources where they are needed.

The United States has been one of the countries that has demonstrated a very real (although limited) compassion ministry to the world. During times of crises, the United States has helped provide for less privileged nations around the world through various portals of compassion and hope. Despite the fact that the United States has also failed repeatedly in this very area, God has nonetheless sustained the nation because of His divine compassion.

Those in the wake of judgment, who sense a covenant with Heaven, will cry out to God, because they will see His love demonstrated in a supernatural way. Types and shadows of this are being mimicked in the secular arenas that are shrouded by humanism. But as the Kingdom age approaches, God's remnant will have learned how to more effectively and efficiently steward resources, bringing relief and comfort to a lost and dying world.

When Jesus paid the ultimate price on the cross, every force in the universe was subsumed under His jurisdiction. Every natural dynamic was forced to submit to God's spiritual laws. Jesus won back the keys to the kingdoms of earth. As His followers, we can begin to operate in accordance with His higher authority—an authority birthed from His heart of justice and mercy in Heaven.

As time grows nearer to Jesus' second coming, we will see a major emphasis on the justice system by both God and the demonic realm. A full reversal of many demonic decrees will arise. At the same time, the enemy will create new—and sometimes darker—edicts. The book of Revelation clearly illustrates this. Demonic forces appear to gain ground, but then where God advances His own purpose, the enemy is quickly thwarted. A war is in play for Heaven's justice system to prevail, and Christians will be pivotal in influencing governmental justice in the nations and also the Church.

AMERICA'S CIVIL RIGHTS MOVEMENT

In January 2001, the Lord instructed me to turn on the television during my daily devotions with Him. At the time, I was on a media fast—avoiding television and movies for a season—so I was shocked that He would so clearly drop that in my heart. I tried to resist, shoving the thought aside as a carnal urge. But after a few seconds, my devotional time grew completely flat. So I ran to the television and turned it on, trying to be obedient to His prompting.

A news program was broadcasting a piece about a well-known minister and political advocate, who was addressing leaders from Kansas City about civil rights. Suddenly, the Lord's audible voice filled the room:

> "This man is touching one of the most precious issues of My heart in America—the civil rights movement. But he is trying to stir it with his own agenda. Because of this, I am about to decrease his voice of authority in the land. If he does not repent within two weeks, I am going to expose nationally a great moral failure of an adulterous affair he is having. After that, if he still does not repent, he will pay even more dearly as I strip away very precious things to him, and he will become a shell of a man."

A trembling fear of the Lord rippled through me, but through this experience, I began to understand the Lord's justice. Here was a man who claimed to influence the nation on behalf of the Church, but he had a very selfish agenda. His speaking was distorted and his impartation corrupted by his own immorality.

God Himself cares so much for the civil rights issues in America that He could no longer let this man go on dishonoring Him. Therefore, God was going to allow this man to be publicly exposed so people would know he was not serving God's agenda.

I shared this word in Kansas City with only a handful of pastors and leaders. The word gave a time frame—within two weeks God was going to expose a moral failure in this man. Even more specifically, God would not let this man's voice stir up the demonic struggle in our city, where the enemy has such a stronghold of racism and oppression between people groups.

Two weeks later in mid-January, newscasts around America featured a young woman with whom this man had had an adulterous affair; he was fully exposed. He admitted to it. When this happened, we were sad for this man and his circumstances, but we also rejoiced that God was taking some measure of authority in our city over the civil rights movement. God cares about justice more then we ever could! This was one of the most graphic pictures of heavenly justice to me, and I was marked by the severe love of God in my spirit.

As we encounter and become involved with Heaven's purposes, God will use believers of every culture to proclaim His heart upon the earth. The power unleashed by this union will be akin to a spiritual atom bomb—shaking everything that can be shaken.

AN EMERGING GENERATION

A generation of young people is about to emerge who will struggle with the lack of heavenly justice more than any other generation. They will not be another cause-oriented generation, such as the one birthed in the seventies. Instead, they will be a generation who cries out for the recompense of Jesus to be delivered to Him.

A profound hunger will hit this entire generation, and they will raise an angry outcry at the lack of justice. The groaning in their hearts will be heard perhaps as prayers before God's throne and will be unparalleled in passion and impact—very much like the cries of the children of Israel in Egypt. So oppressed were the Jews in bondage and slavery, their prayers were inward groans, and the Bible says their silent cries were heard in Heaven.

Likewise, the cries of this generation will join with those laboring for the purpose of Jesus' return—the cloud of witnesses and the martyrs who bring their case before God's throne day and night. An agreement between Heaven and earth is engendered from this synchronicity, because Jesus longs to pour out the very thing for which hearts in Heaven and earth are crying out.

COMING DOMINION OF WEALTH

The Church, especially in the Western world, has had such a corrupt focus on prosperity and financial gain that God has had to discipline us because of our self-centered and self-seeking motives.

God has birthed a true Kingdom prosperity message on the earth, but it is often shrouded by a demonic communiqué.

This false prosperity message especially shows its holes and weaknesses when translated to third world countries where it just doesn't work, at least not in the way it has been promoted by some of its more vocal believers.

Biblical theology carries truth that is relevant in any culture, rich or poor. The prosperity message of the Faith movement did not hold biblical weight in every culture. Although the core of the prosperity message held many truths, the overall picture was centered around self-seeking gain.

In the 1980s and '90s, many mainstream ministries fell because of their lack of integrity with money. Other ministries lost influence because they exploited their followers. As a result, much of the Church has abandoned the prosperity doctrine.

Yet God wants to bring a prosperity message to earth for His covenant people so that He will receive His recompense. If we will purify the motive of the prosperity message, it truly carries a spiritual weightiness. Even people in the poorest nations can begin to steward resources from Heaven's storehouse, if it is by a supernatural manifestation that will bring Jesus His reward.

A COMMANDED BLESSING

When we are united in the priestly purpose for which Jesus entreated His Father in John 17, this releases a commanded blessing from Heaven.

How good and pleasant it is
when brothers live together in unity!
It is like precious oil poured on the head,
running down on the beard,
running down on Aaron's beard,

down upon the collar of his robes.
It is as if the dew of Hermon
were falling on Mount Zion.
For there the LORD bestows his blessing,
even life forevermore.

—PSALM 133

It's not just unity in purpose to one another but union also with Heaven that commands this blessing.

COMMON MISCONCEPTIONS

Major misunderstandings abound among Christians regarding Heaven's justice and financial system. I will try to define a few of them briefly so we can better understand how to position our hearts closer to the One we love.

1. *If I suffer greatly in poverty, then I deserve a payback here on earth.*

God asks us to pay the price of suffering. As payback for our sacrifice, we often begin looking to gain in visible ways. But no earthly payback can compare to what we are going to gain with Christ in Heaven.

If He asks us to pay a price now, we begin to store up a reward in Heaven. Part of His extreme justice is that we will reap from our sacrifice throughout all eternity. Sometimes our sacrifice may birth a higher place of fellowship with Him, which is the goal of those who love Him righteously.

I consider that our present sufferings are not worth comparing with the glory that will be revealed in us.

—ROMANS 8:18

2. If I recognize the enemy's scheme and catch the thief by breaking the devil's power, then I will receive back sevenfold in my finances.

God never promised us a sevenfold return of money. However, this Scripture is rightfully used many times to break off a poverty spirit.

We are sowing into a relationship with Jesus for His sake. If the enemy steals from us, we have the right to plunder him. This can take place in several different ways, but it never follows our expectations.

> Yet if he is caught, he must pay sevenfold,
> though it costs him all the wealth of his house.
> —PROVERBS 6:31

When the enemy steals from us, he is robbing God. This means our witness against the enemy gives God the right to release a larger recompense from the enemy to Jesus. This will manifest in our lives as well, but there is no set way of how it will happen.

What makes this relationship beautiful is that God is creative, and He uses us to break down unrighteousness so that His justice can be released.

Picture it this way: If the enemy started out with seven million dollars and stole one million from you, then he would have to give up the eight million dollars—all he owned. The enemy stole the hearts of two humans in the Garden, but through the redemption of the cross, Jesus has inherited billions of souls—those who were born under sin and darkness and who the enemy had claimed. Now that's justice!

When we discern the enemy's schemes and shut the door to him, we can then open a door for Heaven's justice to burst forth and maximize the return—but we have to be focused on Jesus getting His redemption first. Our incentive can't be first for our own payback, but if we understand God's heavenly agenda of restoring to Jesus what is His, then we will not be afraid to serve this agenda before serving our own. The person who catches the thief who stole from the King will be richly rewarded when he or she turns in the thief.

3. *If I tithe ten percent, then I will get a hundredfold return in my finances.*

We tithe as an act of joining our value system to Heaven's and as a declaration that we belong to God. We are sowing into Jesus' very purposes. So when you give, you may not receive a hundred times back in the specific area you gave, but you will definitely open yourself to be richly blessed in ways that are beyond money.

God is not fixated on paying humans back solely in financial arenas. If He were, many would squander the wealth and be destroyed by it. The stronger need may be in less tangible areas like love, health, relationships, discipline, wisdom, knowledge, skill, etc.

When we give financially, it releases the blessings of favor upon us. This divine favor can manifest itself through many different types of provision. We cannot think of it through the filter of an earthly monetary system; otherwise we will not understand when God is with us—working in us and through us, and even for us.

If our sacrifice ties us to the King's value system, He can then meet us more deeply in whatever way He sees fit—and not just in our felt needs. God sometimes meets us in ways we don't understand because His ways are not our ways. He wants to go beyond our needs and prepare us for spending eternity with Him. Remember that where our treasure is, our heart can be found also. This is why it's so important to give in monetary ways that require great sacrifice.

The ten-percent model is only one part of the New-Covenant model. Under the New Covenant, God wants to possess us fully. That means everything we have is His, and He can require it for His purposes anytime He deems.

I know many business leaders who are being led by God to give a huge percentage of their income—even up to seventy percent. It would seem to be in Heaven's best interest to keep these leaders successful because of their obedient hearts. But God may want to use these leaders in a totally different function; nothing is assured in our lifetime.

God may even ask us to pour out our wealth as an offering, as Mary poured out the costly nard from the alabaster jar (Matthew 26:6–13). Or He may want to prosper us so that we can fund outreaches to the uttermost parts of the earth.

If we were called to give *just* ten percent, then we would not be responsible to God for the rest of our money. We could become separated from His desire. Because we have a covenant with Jesus through the Holy Spirit, the anointing of His relationship confirms that *everything* we have is His.

Actually, this frees us to demand every provision we need in a much fuller way, because we are His and our lack is His lack. Consequently, we must embrace this sacrificial model so our lives themselves are His to do with as He sees fit; He can make a claim on our money or our very lives anytime He wants. Therefore, we can be stewards of more than we ever had, because God will know what we consider His by our actions, not just our intentions. When the enemy steals from us, God will immediately act on our behalf because He cannot deny Himself.

For New-Covenant Christians, the ten-percent model is only a starting point for our giving to God. It is a minimum standard that trains us how to be sacrificial. But as we mature, we will find ourselves sacrificing much more than finances. All our provisions will find their way into His hands for His service.

CHAPTER EIGHT

THE TREASURY
OF GOD

Can plunder be taken from warriors,
or captives rescued from the fierce?

But this is what the LORD says:

"Yes, captives will be taken from warriors,
and plunder retrieved from the fierce;
I will contend with those who contend with you,
and your children I will save."

—ISAIAH 49:24–25

At the age of eighteen, a friend named James went into a trance in which he was transported to a horrific spiritual site. People were chained against walls and writhing in pain. Precious gold, which he knew belonged to the Lord, was locked up in boxes. Demons were holding on to prophetic promises that clearly belonged to Jesus. James wondered where he was, and he was shown that this deeply oppressed place was a treasury of God that had been captured and laid up in the second Heaven.

At first this confused him, since such bondage prevailed there, as if the enemy owned all these people, resources, and callings that clearly belonged to God. James began to intercede—praying that the enemy would return what was rightfully the Lord's—and he began to exhibit an unusual spiritual authority that was beyond his eighteen years. He clinched an agreement with the God of Heaven, and God began to answer his prayers.

The enemy will do whatever he can to ensnare and enslave. He cannot create anything (except trouble and confusion); he must depend on our weak human will to compromise or crack the door open to sin—and then he pounces on this opening and uses it to his own advantage.

The enemy operates covertly and insidiously just like the terrorists involved in the tragedy of September 11, 2001. These terrorists didn't use new technology to destroy the World Trade Center towers. They didn't smuggle in weapons of mass destruction because they probably didn't have access to them. What they did do was strategize to employ our own weapons against us. They attended American flight schools and learned the American flight-navigation system. Then they hijacked four of our own planes to wreak massive destruction and weaken our country with the threat of terror.

The enemy is the master of exploitation and deception. He wants to use the very vehicles of ministry against the beautiful, precious treasure God is birthing. The enemy uses nine parts truth mixed with one part lie and spreads his dominion by having those who would compromise agree with these deceptions.

It's truly amazing how crafty Satan can be with the short leash and limited resources God has allowed him. God never gave him anything. Satan gains ground and influence by manipulating and controlling humans to whom God has given talents, gifts, and a measure of grace for success.

So what happens when God begins to awaken hearts around the world? What happens when an entire generation begins to come into agreement with God rather than agreement with their sinful desires? The enemy is displaced, because his only tools and resources are what humans forfeit through sin.

This is why God hated Esau; he despised and forfeited his inheritance, which belonged not only to Esau but also to the Ruler of Heaven. When we despise our gifts and talents, we despise God Himself. We come into agreement with our own flesh, which empowers the enemy to work through our gifts and abilities. Even some who are viewed by others as mature Christians are guilty of despising their spiritual inheritances.

The bigger picture, on the other hand, is that God has a Kingdom at His disposal. He has never lost to the enemy—not even a portion of what was significant to Him. Plus, God has the ability to create, inspire, and bear fruit. There's no doubt that it must make the enemy jealous when God grants humans success and fruitfulness. It must also be a great disappointment to God when His children try to imitate the lesser, worldly fruitfulness arising from manipulation and deceit.

The key to gaining entry into Heaven's storehouse and reclaiming what belongs to God is to align ourselves with His will and agree with Him about what is His. If we stop forfeiting our rights and abandon ourselves to Him, we will attain all that He has available to us.

GIFT OF A ROLEX WATCH

After my second visitation from the Minister of Finance, I awoke the next morning to find the family with whom I was staying up and about. Their youngest son greeted me, full of excitement. "Shawn, I had a dream about you last night," he said. "A man gave you a watch and it was a Rolex. He said you would be able to tell new time on it!"

This seven-year-old's dream pierced my heart. I had seen a Rolex watch only a few times in my life. I could almost remember a distinguishing feature on the watch face: a crown insignia. Quite honestly, I couldn't have cared less about the actual Rolex brand, but the symbolic picture of the Rolex was beautiful to me. Then in my spirit I heard the Lord say, "I am crowning your time with My purpose." I didn't understand this statement, but it sounded poetic and elegant, and in my heart, I exulted in what He said; it felt like an invitation.

Two months later, I spoke at a conference in Idaho. When I returned home, I received a call from the conference host. She asked, "Do you remember that watch we received in the offering? Everyone prayed and felt you were to have it. Did you pray about it?"

Taken by surprise, I asked, "What watch?" This was new revelation to me; I hadn't heard anything about it.

"Didn't I tell you?" she replied. "It's a Rolex watch. We had it appraised and it's real. We feel we are supposed to give it to you. Has God spoken anything to you about a watch?"

I was shocked. Having a Rolex meant nothing to me in the natural, but the spiritual point God was making was huge. It seemed as if God were summoning something from the seven-year-old's dream into reality, making a serious point. I remembered the two phrases I had heard: *You are going to learn how to tell new time*, and *I am crowning your time with My purpose.*

She offered to hand-deliver the watch to me at another conference in Albany, Oregon, where I was scheduled to speak.

At first I didn't tell anyone; I was shocked by the news. Then two weeks before I was to receive the watch, I attended a meeting in Kansas City at the International House of Prayer. A woman I didn't know approached me and prophesied:

> "I see God putting a Rolex watch on your wrist. It is gold and silver. He is doing this because He is going to accelerate your time. It's a gold and silver watch. It represents the resources from Heaven coming to you in an accelerated way to accomplish all that He has put in your heart."

This woman had not heard my Rolex story. I had told *only* three people in a private way. I was flabbergasted!

Suddenly, it struck me that I had never asked her to describe the Rolex. I didn't actually know what a Rolex looked like; I couldn't really remember the one or two I had seen. So that night I called her and shared the prophetic word with her. She told me that the Rolex was gold and silver and had a crown on its face. I was so amazed at how God was using this natural item to drive home a spiritual point.

SPIRIT OF ESAU

When I received the watch, I was in awe that God had actually brought the word to me again through an object. He was making an extravagant point on purpose by using a watch that speaks of status to the world but only of the crowning of time to me. My first notion was to sell the watch to obtain extra provision for our ministry or even as an additional gift for the poor. I explored ways to sell it and was almost ready to when I received a strong rebuke from the Lord:

"Esau sold His inheritance out of the need for provision [in other words, he was hungry], and I hated him. Will you do the same to Me?"

Ouch! I realized the Lord had given me a token of His love and a prophetic sign in the natural realm. He wanted the watch to serve as a prophetic symbol to me. Then He told me:

"You are called to possess in the natural realm. The only time it becomes dangerous is when you are satisfied with what you possess and grow content. Everything that is inspired by My Spirit for your possession will only cause you to press on even more toward the highest goal of dwelling with Me."

My heart was overwhelmed. The watch changed my entire perspective and became precious—not as a treasure in its worldly value, lest it be an idol. It did not hold value as a memento, either, lest I build an altar and grow content. Rather, the watch's value to me was in its display of how real God's love is and how much more I need of His love. It put a drive in me toward my heavenly goal of being with Him.

God does not want to limit us in possessing the accoutrements of this world. However, He demands that ultimately they must draw us to Him. If they do not, they will distract us and push us away from Him. Remember: Our heart lies where our treasure is.

One day God may require me to give away the watch, which I actually look forward to if He does. It's His. It has served me in the sense of being a palpable demonstration of His love and communication toward me. Besides, nothing on earth is permanent; we are less than eternal on this plane.

Nevertheless, God did give it to me, and until then I will steward it with gratitude.

BLINDSIDED BY PRIDE

Many believe they have earned possessions from God's treasury by their own strength, skill, and power. They worked hard; they were driven; they made it happen. People who are susceptible to deception read statements like this and ruminate self-righteously: *How awful that others believe they are responsible for their own strength. I'm glad I don't believe that.*

But these same individuals fall into the pride of life. The last time I was deceived, I had no idea I had veered from the truth—that's the whole point of deceit.

We are drawing closer to Jesus' return. Although it may not be tomorrow, it is soon. The fear of the Lord should grip us. Since we are nearer to that decisive hour, God is releasing to His covenant people the ability to produce wealth like never before. God is confirming His covenant both to Jesus and to us.

Many have tasted success and have let their pride blind them into believing that success came through their own giftings and talents. It's uncannily easy to lose our desperation for Jesus to inherit what is His when our circumstances cushion us with creature comforts.

Solomon fell into this trap, and he is considered the wisest man in all of history. How could he, who had so much wisdom, settle for less than the highest Kingdom purpose? It happened because of one thing: Solomon grew content. He lost his desperation for eternity and focused on earthly pleasures. That tells me that the strongest pleasures on earth can be a perfect counterfeit even to the wisest of the wise. We have to be on guard not to settle for the earthly even when it feels spiritual.

God is sincere in His intentions and will not tolerate pride in those whom He is entrusting with His investment into His Son's inheritance. I used the following Scripture earlier, but let's look at it again:

> So he said to me, "This is the word of the LORD to Zerubbabel: 'Not by might nor by power, but by my Spirit,' says the LORD Almighty."
>
> —ZECHARIAH 4:6

The Spirit of God was encouraging Zerubbabel to complete the building of the temple while recognizing it was God who was empowering the man, not his own skills or abilities. When it comes to building God's temple, He spares no expense. He will not cease to empower those He has called to the task. It is a holy stewardship of purpose.

DIVINE INCENTIVES

Bobby Conner, a friend and prophetic voice, goes so far as to say that God releases in us the *incentive* for stewardship. When David inquired of the men of Israel and discovered that the man who slew Goliath would receive wealth, the king's daughter, and tax exemptions (1 Samuel 17:25), this was a great incentive to kill the giant who stood in the way of God's covenant people.

And as I mentioned earlier, when Solomon built the temple, there was enough provision left over for him to build himself a stupendous palace. Sometimes we may receive personal gain as we pave the way for God's higher purposes. He richly rewards us, but our rewards cannot be our sole focus or preoccupation.

David would have killed Goliath even if he had not been offered an incentive. We know this because he had already killed both a lion and a bear that were trying to attack the flock of sheep he was tending. In killing Goliath, David had the added incentive of Saul's offer; this only compelled him further to learn more of God's goodness.

God gives us the reward of Jesus on top of the great reward waiting in Heaven, all the while sending us spiritual postcards as reminders to empower our passion. These incentives do not substitute our passion, but they bring zeal as described by David:

Zeal for your house consumes me.

—Psalm 69:9

When the Lord offered to give Solomon anything he wanted, Solomon understood that the incentive was not the focus. Instead of asking to steward wealth or power, he asked God for wisdom and discernment:

The Lord was pleased that Solomon had asked for this. So God said to him, "Since you have asked for this and not for long life or wealth for yourself, nor have asked for the death of your enemies but for discernment in administering justice, I will do what you have asked. I will give you a wise and discerning heart, so that there will never have been anyone like you, nor will there ever be."

—1 Kings 3:10–12

Even Jesus benefited from an incentive as He was able to wholeheartedly obey the Father: He obeyed first for the

Father's pleasure and then for the inheritance that was promised to Him.

MOTIVES OF STEWARDSHIP

I believe God is beckoning a generation who would not have any agenda other than to discern His heart—just as Solomon had asked. God is declaring our generation to be unlike any other generation on the face of the earth. Zeal for God does not limit our stewardship; it demands more responsibility and offers the privilege of partnering with Heaven.

Surveying past generations, we are assured that wealth is *not* the answer. Nor is resource. Only the unhindered presence of the Holy Spirit abiding in our lives can satisfy our inner longings. When we are as desperate for God's heart as Paul was, we will attract the abundance that is drawn to our dependence on God. Then, to the degree He can trust us, God can release stewardship.

One day as I was praying, God mentioned something to me I had never considered. He shared:

"I enjoy stewarding the resources of Heaven and earth. I have created humans in My own image, with the same enjoyment of stewardship."

Did you realize that God created us to enjoy stewarding money? He created us to take great pleasure in managing possessions. This principle gets thoroughly lacerated by the demonic, and the religious spirit of the Church displaces it. As His bride, Jesus intends stewardship to not *just* be a test to assess and grow character in us; He wants us to enjoy partnering with Him in finances and resources.

It is true that once one begins to have a flow of resources, it actually complicates life rather than simplifies it. Everyone who has wants more, because more is required to support the wealth one has already acquired.

At the same time, having resources at one's disposal allows for the possibility of weilding greater authority, responsibility, and, consequently, a different level of partnership in Kingdom resources.

Many people cry out for more without considering the consequences. God knows He cannot always give us what we want, because we may not be ready for the responsibility, even though we may feel we are—it could ruin us. If God multiplied your business' income and influence, you would need more employees, equipment, and a larger workspace. Or if God moved your church to a larger building, more expenses would be required to maintain it. The more you steward, the more responsibility is demanded.

To whom much is given, much is required. If we are stewarding God's treasury for Jesus' sake, how much more responsibility is entailed in holding the keys to that very treasury. Each individual is accountable before the throne for how he or she has used Heaven's resources. Don't be manipulated into bowing before a human altar by seeking to please your neighbor instead of God.

RESPONSIBILITY OF WEALTH

Think about the mighty responsibility of stewardship on the rich. I know a godly man who has started several multimillion-dollar companies and has become one of the wealthiest men in his city.

Each year, he receives tens of thousands of letters from

those in real need—from missionaries in other countries to single mothers who will never have the money to pay for surgeries their children need. These needs keep him on his knees in prayer, asking God, "How do I steward Your money?" He is a man after God's own heart, because he truly knows it is God's wealth.

CAUTION FOR GOD'S LEADERS

I am about to address a dangerous subject, because it can be so imbalanced. Too often people blame others—especially leadership—for their problems.

But another dilemma faces the Body of Christ. Several prominent Church leaders have stewarded the Church's finances with wrong motives. They have used the Kingdom's good cause to exploit people—not to build the Kingdom but their own agendas.

In the last decade, Christian individuals, churches, and ministries had hundreds of millions of dollars embezzled through investment schemes. Several well-known and influential men and women in ministry were seduced into business opportunities that were illegitimate. Many ministries actually raised money from their local congregations or their support networks to invest more money into these opportunities, which came to nothing.

How can we protect ourselves from such schemes? It's so simple: *You will know those who serve God by their fruit.* A man or woman who is stewarding resources wisely will produce fruit of radical passion, souls saved, miracles, training and equipping—meaning, they will reproduce disciples—and they will have provision.

Churches in the Body of Christ need to be very open and

honest in the financial arena; they need to uphold a godly standard of integrity, not a worldly one. Most leaders in the Body of Christ who are entrusted with stewarding finances have sincere and noble hearts to do good, accomplish the will of God, and love people. In contrast, the ministries that end up taking advantage of their supporters sound like they have good intentions, but they usually have a lack of accountability because of impure motives.

Truth be told, there are hundreds of thousands of leaders, and not all are accountable to their congregations or walking in God's will. It's not every churchgoer's responsibility to correct this—it is God's. However, it is our responsibility as churchgoers to "know" the men and women who are leading us, so we serve only the cause of those to whom we are called.

For example, let's say your income or business profits are hundreds of millions every year and you go to a small local church that has one-hundred-plus members. If you steward your entire ten-percent tithe to that one congregation, it could be millions a year. Let's say their budget is just under a few hundred thousand dollars; the additional money that could be a blessing could also immediately ruin the church if it doesn't have the vision or character to steward the finances properly. For those the Lord blesses with wealth, there must be a building of trust with the ministry organizations that are receiving the tithes and offerings. This is hard to hear for some ministries, but the distribution of wealth is something that an individual is highly accountable to before God.

Some dear friends of mine whom God has blessed with wealth felt called to give financially to several places, but the pastor told them they were not following a biblical model and God would put them under a curse for robbing the church. These poor people, who by themselves were giving away far more than all the other church members combined, were so confused that a heavy yoke came upon them as a result. So against the leading of the Holy Spirit, they gave all to the pastor. Needless to say, within a year the church fell apart, and the pastor was exposed for adultery and had laundered a large amount of money from the church account.

RED FLAGS

When any person tries to control your finances or resources by manipulation rather than inspiration, a prominent red flag should flash a warning in your heart. If God is offering you stewardship over resources big or small, you must do two things:

1. Give whatever percentage God directs to support the ministry or church family to which you belong, and let it be a *free* gift—with no strings attached.
2. Be accountable to steward His finances with wisdom and discernment.

What if God is calling you to be an apostle of finance? What if He is training you to partner with His purpose to fund and build structures of the Kingdom, as well as give to others who would build?

Others are not called to steward your resources for you. It is a false witness in the Church that prompts us to lay all of our finances down at apostles' feet so they can build with our resources. It could be that God is calling *you* to be an apostle of finance. What if He is training you to partner with His purpose to fund and build structures that a ministry-minded person cannot see?

My friends who gave so much money to their church

entered into a gross error. For one couple to be responsible for the church's entire income put them in a compromising position. What if the husband's work required them to move? Their church may have collapsed because of its dependence on a person. In addition, if their pastor already had an excess of money and could not grow his church past one hundred after several years, why would God want this couple to invest more finances into a structure lacking vision? Because of bad doctrine, this couple had a false sense of responsibility to give to that one place.

God has placed within each one of us the desire to steward resources. All civilization revolves around this. It is not a carnal desire rooted in materialism and greed; it is a spiritually based desire. God wants us to enjoy stewarding the resources He has given us.

For the love of money is a root of all kinds of evil.
Some people, eager for money, have wandered from
the faith and pierced themselves with many griefs.
—1 TIMOTHY 6:10

Although it is commonly misquoted, Scripture does not say that money *is* evil. Money, like any other provision, is neutral. Rather, it is the attitude of the heart—greed, fear, and anxiety—toward money that determines whether it is good or evil.

God is searching beyond the formats, structures, and programs we call *religion*. He is looking past the walls, divisions, and definitions humans have established to worship Him. God loves buildings and people, but His eyes range to and fro, encompassing the entire world as His inheritance. God is scrutinizing hearts and character to find stewards for His resources and people who would be vessels for a greater measure of the Spirit so they can fulfill the desires of His heart.

As lovers of God, we should join together to make every sacrifice with our money, service, and love—without placing a price tag on what we give. The reality is that our love will motivate us to give. If we refrain from obediently giving a regular hefty percentage of our money in a sacrificial lifestyle—usually much more than ten percent—then we will be opening ourselves to the enemy's oppression in our finances. How much of a percentage of our resources—and what is considered "sacrificial"—is individual and flows from our personal relationship with the Lord.

I don't believe God judges us for *not* giving. But when we give, we open the door for God to move in the natural realm—in our character, lifestyle, finances, health, and many other areas. When we do not give sacrificially, our treasure becomes limited to what we receive on earth, because we haven't opened the door for God to move through this avenue, which is so important to Him.

CHAPTER NINE

THE DOUBLE-PORTION ANOINTING

Return to your fortress, O prisoners of hope;
even now I announce that I will restore twice as
much to you.

—*ZECHARIAH 9:12*

A man came to my office seeking a consultation about his life. Struggling financially, he believed he was called to ministry, but he was unable to support himself living on the small donations he received. As I prayed for him, I perceived that God had placed a deliverance gift in his hands. But God was also giving him a business strategy for the Internet and sought to use his technological skill to provide for him. When I told him this, he became defensive: "But I gave up all my skills and career to follow Jesus; now I am living by faith."

"No, God has given you this ability," I reminded him, "and ministry is not just in the four walls of the Church. He is calling you, but not exclusively to the Church."

"You mean like a tent-making business?" he asked, referring to the apostle Paul.

Suddenly, I realized how twisted the average Christian's perspective has become regarding those in secular jobs; we tend to think they are second-class citizens of the Kingdom.

So I replied, "No, God has not given you a tent-making ability. He's given you a double-portion anointing. You are called to build the Kingdom, ministering in power to the Church. You are also called to inspire new ways for Christians to prepare Internet Web pages, creating formats for many people to get their messages out to both the Church and world markets. Through this, you will come in contact with many people Jesus loves but no one else is pursuing, and you will be His mouthpiece to them. It's not an either/or choice—it's both/and!"

Immediately, he felt a great spiritual weightiness, and he knew this was God's presence. His mind was freed from striving for a wrong identity in his personal calling.

The provision was in his hands, just like the rod was in Moses' hand.

A DIVINE WAKE-UP CALL

One night a shrilling alarm woke me from a deep sleep. Groggily checking the nightstand, I realized I didn't have any alarm set in my room. The sound had pealed from Heaven and God was waking me up. He told me:

"There is about to be a massive wake-up call in the Body of Christ. I am calling a hopeless generation to abide in Me. As they come by the masses, they will inherit not only as sons but also as the bride of

Christ. It is a double-portion inheritance to be stewarded even now on earth."

Favor graces those who shine under Heaven's light. Scripture reminds us:

And you will be called priests of the LORD,
you will be named ministers of our God.
You will feed on the wealth of nations,
and in their riches you will boast.

Instead of their shame
my people will receive a double portion,
and instead of disgrace
they will rejoice in their inheritance;
and so they will inherit a double portion in their land,
and everlasting joy will be theirs.

—ISAIAH 61:6–7

In the last days, God wants to raise up a remnant of people who will reflect the testimony of Joseph recorded in the book of Genesis. Joseph was born into favor with his father, but his brothers were jealous. Through his long, persecuted, and sacrificial journey, Joseph ended up serving Pharaoh and was set in charge of a large portion of the kingdom. His position enabled him to provide for God's people, Israel, in generous ways that would have been impossible had he not been appointed for this role.

Joseph was not just chosen by Pharaoh for a significant leadership role; he had also grown in favor with God and was appointed to a heavenly leadership role over God's covenant people. Like the prophet Samuel, Joseph grew in favor with

God first and humanity second. This afforded him a role with humanity and then with God and God's people.

Joseph is a parabolic picture of how God is asking many to pay a price right now. Joseph paid a great price, and many times he wondered why God allowed such great calamity in his life. Because Joseph kept his heart right no matter how bad the circumstances, he always rose to favor in whatever environment he found himself—whether in Potiphar's house, in jail, or with Pharaoh. This serves as a paradigm for God's covenant people and the favor apportioned to us on the earth. God also wants to grant His covenant people influence and favor even in the midst of suffering. It's time to seize God's promises.

He has guided many along this journey of obedience so that at the right time, they can be raised up in the midst of the famine of creativity and the wilderness of barrenness that will overshadow the world during the end times. As I mentioned earlier, the great grace that has enveloped the Western world has seemed so common that we have been inclined to take it for granted. Yet one day God will lift off this great grace, and only what is spiritually powered by God or the enemy will prosper. Human effort will achieve nothing; people will have to choose whom to serve. When that time arrives, those with a Joseph anointing will be entrusted with a significant stewardship of blessing, in order that all Jesus' purposes may not fail to be fulfilled for lack of resources.

MINISTERING TO THE POOR

When the Minister of Finance first visited me, he showed me a mighty monetary move that would begin to heal the hungry and poor of the earth. One of the most direct and powerful ways for believers in the Western world to agree with the

Minister of Finance and see Heaven's resources move into their lives is to pray for a heart for the earth's poor.

In my second experience with the Minister of Finance, he advised me:

> "When you love those who are not loved, you gain a
> greater authority. When you love them in tangible
> ways such as feeding them, clothing them, caring for
> them, visiting them, adopting them, then you can
> accelerate God's activity in other areas of your life. It
> opens the Heavens over you, just like it provided Jesus
> a greater influence when He touched the poor and
> afflicted of the earth. When Jesus touched the poor
> and the weak and made them whole by His love,
> some of the greatest levels of Heaven's ministry ever
> known to humanity were brought to earth, and God's
> light increased throughout the world. Imitate this!"

The Minister of Finance then led me to the book of Isaiah:

> "Is not this the kind of fasting I have chosen:
> to loose the chains of injustice
> and untie the cords of the yoke,
> to set the oppressed free
> and break every yoke?
> Is it not to share your food with the hungry
> and to provide the poor wanderer with shelter—
> when you see the naked, to clothe him,
> and not to turn away from your own flesh and blood?
> Then your light will break forth like the dawn,
> and your healing will quickly appear;
> then your righteousness will go before you,

and the glory of the LORD will be your rear guard.
Then you will call, and the LORD will answer;
you will cry for help, and he will say: Here am I.

"If you do away with the yoke of oppression,
with the pointing finger and malicious talk,
and if you spend yourselves in behalf of the hungry
and satisfy the needs of the oppressed,
then your light will rise in the darkness,
and your night will become like the noonday.
The LORD will guide you always;
he will satisfy your needs in a sun-scorched land
and will strengthen your frame.
You will be like a well-watered garden,
like a spring whose waters never fail.
Your people will rebuild the ancient ruins
and will raise up the age-old foundations;
you will be called Repairer of Broken Walls,
Restorer of Streets with Dwellings."

—ISAIAH 58:6–12

This passage provides the greatest key to spiritual acceleration and growing in favor with God and humanity. God's move to redistribute and multiply finances and resources will continue and escalate among His followers until the earthly climax of the end times, when God will use His body to channel great wealth and resources to His purposes for the nation of Israel.

So, it starts with the poor. Based on what this compassionate angel revealed to me, I don't believe anyone can truly prosper in God's Kingdom without a heart for the poor.

CHAPTER TEN

EXTRAVAGANT GIVING

*Command them to do good, to be rich in good deeds,
and to be generous and willing to share. In this way
they will lay up treasure for themselves as a firm
foundation for the coming age, so that they may take
hold of the life that is truly life.*

—*1 TIMOTHY 6:18–19*

While I was at a conference in Canada, the angelic Minister of Finance was sent once again to help me understand more revelation about Heaven's economy. This time, he informed me:

"The Lord is going to inspire the Macedonian example. It will take the Macedonian lifestyle to enter into the higher purposes He is proposing for this generation."

I searched through the Bible and saw that Paul was exposed to Macedonian generosity that flowed from extreme poverty. He wrote:

And now, brothers, we want you to know about the grace that God has given the Macedonian churches. Out of the most severe trial, their overflowing joy and their extreme poverty welled up in rich generosity. For I testify that they gave as much as they were able, and even beyond their ability.

—2 CORINTHIANS 8:1–3

Then the Minister of Finance stated:

"The Holy Spirit is going to lead the Church to give in ways that are impossible according to human nature. God wants you to give according to the desire of Jesus' heart. This heart attitude describes a people who give beyond their own ability, spoken about by Paul."

This type of giving is completely foreign to the Western world; we give humanistically—when our hearts are touched with compassion or when we are inspired by visible affliction. However, once these issues are forgotten, atrocities escape the Western world's conscience and attention.

God is calling for a people who would build their storehouse in Heaven. He is seeking a people who have a reworked eternal-value structure that does not revolve around the world's economy.

Jesus' burning desire is so threatening to those who "possess" anything—whether it be wealth or not—that many encounter the heart of this beautiful Man only to depart like the rich man who asked Jesus how to enter eternity:

Jesus answered, "If you want to be perfect, go, sell your possessions and give to the poor, and you will have treasure in heaven. Then come, follow me."

When the young man heard this, he went away sad, because he had great wealth.

Then Jesus said to his disciples, "I tell you the truth, it is hard for a rich man to enter the kingdom of heaven. Again I tell you, it is easier for a camel to go through the eye of a needle than for a rich man to enter the kingdom of God."

—MATTHEW 19:21–24

This rich man could not give according to Jesus' desire, because his value system was entangled with the world's and cost too much.

We have to learn to give according to God's desire. However, we can only be led to do this through an encounter with the Holy Spirit. People who are stewarding resources for the Kingdom cannot maintain an extravagant heart unless they regularly encounter God's heart. Otherwise, they will become overwhelmed by life's pressures and human predicaments and try to resolve them by human wisdom, which finds its basis in truth, but it is godly understanding applied outside of relationship with God.

Human wisdom leads us according to our own agenda. It does not fulfill Heaven's agenda. Human wisdom can lead us alongside and in sight of the true path, but it does not lead us upon that path.

The rich young man spoken about in Matthew 19 had lived according to the truth of godly wisdom by fulfilling all the Mosaic laws. But when Jesus challenged him to relinquish everything as an extravagant offering of sacrifice and worship, the man couldn't do it. He couldn't fulfill such a request, because he loved his own life too much.

YIELDED TO GOD'S PURPOSES

God is looking for wholehearted vessels to flow through. He will not invest in anything less than those who are fully yielded to Him, because He needs them to live according to His purpose.

The stewardship of resources is one of the greatest tests of wholeheartedness, since every culture on earth in some way revolves around this. In Western culture we establish retirement plans, 401(k)s, social security, savings accounts, and all manner of insurance (some even mandatory). We live with storehouses because of the general grace on our countries. Our cultures are fashioned to build personal security for our future. In such societies, we cannot help but develop mindsets that lead to bondage. It is not a wicked or wrong desire to be secured through these potentially wise means, but God is *not* asking for wisdom first. God wants to see ravished hearts who are devoted to Him and who seek to live a life abandoned to His desire for us.

As believers we are aware of our long-term future, but most of us do not live with a daily desire to invest into it. We are more preoccupied in money and materialism—houses, cars, jobs, financial security, making money, owning, and borrowing. At the same time, God is entreating us, *There is a higher place! Come up here!*

SPIRIT OF ANANIAS AND SAPPHIRA

It doesn't mean we are completely failing God in every aspect and are less than wholehearted if we have kept a little for ourselves; however, if God is asking for everything and we don't give everything but only most, then we are walking a dangerous line. When we come to worship singing, "I surrender all," we are living a lie.

God will not share His glory with anyone, so if we hold on to some assets but pretend to be giving, we are manifesting the same deception that killed Ananias and Sapphira (Acts 5). Ananias and Sapphira sold a field and went to deliver the money for Kingdom building. Ananias laid the money at the apostles' feet, claiming it was all he had made from the sale. Peter rebuked him for lying about his gift and holding part of it back.

This serious transgression resulted in his death and is an example for us. His wife, Sapphira, who wasn't responsible for holding back some of the money, also lied and died as well. This illustrates what happens when we hold back but pretend to be giving everything. The spirit of Ananias and Sapphira is the spirit of this world, which longs to hold ownership over what does not belong to it.

AN INVITATION TO RADICAL GENEROSITY

An awesome invitation is being sent us—the very release of revelation on how to give. Part of what will constitute deliverance for the Western world is when those who have much to lose start taking risks and leaps of faith by giving and sowing extravagantly into God's heart. If you don't know where to give radically to please God, you can find the two largest targets singled out all through the Bible: the poor and the Jewish people.

We can accelerate our spiritual growth by giving to the poor, which partners with God's heart. When we give to Israel, though, we not only accelerate our personal spiritual growth and blessing, but we actually accelerate the Lord's coming.

The only way Israel as a nation will enter into her covenant purpose that has been so clearly prophesied throughout Scripture is for an extravagant heart of giving to come upon Christians. God is going to unite His Christian covenant people with His Jewish covenant people, to whom He has made very clear promises, then completely raze the wall of partition and draw both into His heart. If the Church will partner with Heaven for resources allotted to fulfill God's covenant purposes for Israel, we will accelerate the Lord's coming.

An illustration of this exists over America. One reason there is such a strong grace to prosper over the United States is that President Harry S. Truman and a generation of the American people helped restore Israel as a nation in 1948 by providing resources and protection. This so touched God's heart that it brought great prosperity and an escalation of purpose to America as an entire country.

I guarantee that if other nations support Israel with these types of heavenly strategies, they will be marked for quick advancement in spiritual visitation that does not affect just the Church but their culture's entire society. This is vital to entering into God's end-time purposes.

An awesome invitation exists for those taking on this partnership who are already strategically positioned in a secular prophetic calling. God wants to offer great resources to nations who will extravagantly give, who will help accelerate His purpose in allowing the age to come to manifest now.

CHAPTER ELEVEN

THE DOORWAY OF FAVOR

Now he who supplies seed to the sower and bread for food will also supply and increase your store of seed and enlarge the harvest of your righteousness. You will be made rich in every way so that you can be generous on every occasion, and through us your generosity will result in thanksgiving to God.

—*2 CORINTHIANS 9:10–11*

One night in a dream, I saw a tentacled beast emerge from the ocean. It was like a dragon, with many tentacles coming from its torso. As I studied it, I realized I was seeing the globe, and this beast was as large as a continent. Its tentacles were reaching out and touching many capital cities around the world as well as key commercial sites.

Wherever the tentacles touched, devastation and darkness would befall that society as immorality and lawlessness increased. In each area, though, some sites were shining with light as if they were contained within a protective bubble or sphere. The beast's heavy tentacle could not crush this sphere, however hard it tried.

These "shining ones" seemed to be prospering in more

ways than just wealth; they had happiness, morality, and an atmosphere of Heaven around them. The spheres were positioned in the center of the dragon's activity, which was concentrated on well-populated areas around the world.

Everyone who walked past these light spheres could see inside. Nothing was hidden, and the people outside the spheres would become desperate to imitate what they viewed in the spheres. The only danger was if the people inside the spheres would wander outside these protected places out of curiosity or sin; then they would die, and the radiant sphere would weaken in intensity.

When I awoke, I vaguely understood that this dragon-beast represented the Antichrist spirit that is already at work in the nations. The tentacles' placements showed where this spirit was exercising dominion, and the luminous spheres represented where believers are commissioned to be a greater light amidst great darkness. Since the "shining ones" are called in a very specific way, if they leave their sphere of authority, influence, or relationship, they will not only hurt themselves, but they will also tear down what God has been building.

SPIRIT OF THE WORLD

In the days to come, anyone who chooses to be involved with commerce or business will undoubtedly find him- or herself at war with the spirit of this world—the Antichrist spirit. The Antichrist spirit is going to claim authority over all markets and countries, except wherever God raises up a counterculture.

Our Heavenly Father has specific mandates, which He will give to the people He has chosen. The enemy's influence, no matter how it may look, will never be as high or strong as Jesus Christ's. These chosen ones understand God's purposes and pursue a high call to reach the world. Future generations will *not* have to ask, "What is your calling?" It will be known.

To be overcomers—not just mere survivors—in the days to come, we will need to war with a violent, merciless nature against evil. Even secular positions will need to be pursued with only the highest calling in mind.

CAPTURING HEAVEN'S ATTENTION

When the Minister of Finance left the room the second time and flew up to Heaven, he disappeared through a doorway. I saw a huge gate located in the middle of the heavenly sky. The nameplate across the top of the gate read: THE DOORWAY OF FAVOR.

> It was also the doorway to Isaiah 62:
> You shall no longer be termed Forsaken . . .
> You shall be called Sought Out,
>   A City Not Forsaken.
> —ISAIAH 62:4, 12, NKJV

I knew that this was a doorway that, when passed through, would cause divine favor to be released in Heaven and on earth. Those who entered through this door would capture Heaven's attention. Then, they would be sought after and filled with His abundance.

I also knew that to traverse this doorway, one would have to go on a journey of seeking God the way He desires to be found. One couldn't buy one's way in. One couldn't find a formula to pay one's way in. Only relationship with the Divine brings favor from Heaven and opens this door.

In a small way, I have entered through this door and experienced a mere shadow of the divine favor that is available to us. From the time we enter in, we must be prepared individually or corporately for the changes in people's attitudes toward us: In our interactions on earth, we have Heaven's favor, and we have the hatred of hell. People will no longer be just lukewarm toward us, because we carry such an atmosphere of Heaven that we will have either good or bad interactions.

In essence this happens because we become a heavenly target for God's will. The enemy then tries to set other people's strongholds against God's purpose in your life. Satan tries to use others' weaknesses against you. The good news is that Heaven also begins to touch earth, and unsaved people respond to the love of Heaven that accompanies this state.

RESEMBLING THE FATHER

Earlier in this book, I described how people actually begin to resemble the angelic Minister of Finance as they embrace the calling to become a minister of God's resources on earth. To take this thought one step further, as we come into agreement with the Father's will, we begin to look like Him:

> "I have given them the glory that you gave me, that they may be one as we are one: I in them and you in me . . .
>
> "Father, I want those you have given me to be with me where I am, and to see my glory, the glory you have given me because you loved me before the creation of the world."
>
> —JOHN 17:22, 24

Now we see but a poor reflection as in a mirror; then
we shall see face to face. Now I know in part; then I
shall know fully, even as I am fully known.

—1 CORINTHIANS 13:12

And we, who with unveiled faces all reflect the
Lord's glory, are being transformed into his likeness
with ever-increasing glory, which comes from the
Lord, who is the Spirit.

—2 CORINTHIANS 3:18

As we maintain the Holy Spirit's continued indwelling and
demonstrate obedience to His direction, we become so appeal-
ing to Jesus that we provoke His heart toward us. He draws
near, and His love, righteousness, and power transform us.

PARTNERING WITH GOD

"I know your deeds. See, I have placed before you an
open door that no one can shut. I know that you
have little strength, yet you have kept my word and
have not denied my name."

—REVELATION 3:8

As this revelation of Heaven's economy unfolded to me, I
began to have a desperate longing to partner with the Father's
plan to use every resource—natural and supernatural—to win
Jesus His full reward.

If we really comprehend what is due Him, we can appre-
hend a greater measure of faith to do the works of the Kingdom.